JAMES T. COLBERT

UNDERSTANDING EVOLUTION

Second Edition

UNDERSTANDING
EVOLUTION

E. Peter Volpe
Tulane University

WM. C. BROWN COMPANY PUBLISHERS
Dubuque, Iowa

CONCEPTS OF BIOLOGY SERIES

Consulting Editor
E. Peter Volpe
Tulane University

Copyright ©1967, 1970 by Wm. C. Brown Company Publishers

Library of Congress Catalog Card Number: 76-135419

ISBN 0—697—0413—7

Sixth Printing, 1974

Printed in the United States of America

To My
Ever-Probing Students
Who Taught Me
How to Teach

Biology today is in the midst of profound and exciting revelations. The spectacular surge of biological knowledge has dramatized the need for new approaches to the teaching of biology. The **Concepts of Biology Series,** designed for the introductory course, transmits the excitement of biology to the college student seeking a liberal education. The underlying theme of each book in the series is to foster an awareness of biology as an imaginative, evolving science. While the individual titles are self-contained, collectively they comprise a modern synthesis of major biological principles.

Contents

Preface

This new edition of *Understanding Evolution*, like the previous one, is addressed to students, for whom the book was written. I have endeavored to present a simple, concise account of the scope and significance of evolution for the college student seeking a liberal education. I hope that it may dispel the vague and naive notions about evolution entertained by many beginning students. They look upon evolution as something that has occurred in the remote past. They know it has something to do with dinosaurs, rocks, and the proverbial "missing link." And they are familiar with such alluring clichés as "struggle for existence" and "survival of the fittest." But few pause to consider how the process of evolution actually works. In the belief that any concept can be best understood by knowing how it operates, I have dealt here principally with the mechanism of evolution, the causal aspect rather than the historical. I have given particular attention to modern observations and experiments which illustrate and clarify the evolutionary process. I have used several examples of changes in human populations, so that the student may come to realize that evolution in mankind has not come to a standstill.

Evolution is a process of continual change. Organisms throughout life's history have not remained constant, but have gradually and endlessly changed. Change is the rule of living things. The occurrence of evolution, however, does not in itself reveal *how* evolution is brought about. An event or phenomenon may be known to us and accepted as true, even though the forces that determine its existence may not be fully understood. It scarcely seems necessary to debate the fact that evolution, as an event, has occurred. It is in the *explanation* of evolution that differences of opinion have arisen. One may challenge an interpretation, but to contest the interpretation is not to deny the existence of the event itself. A widespread fallacy is to discredit the truth of evolution by seizing upon points of disagreement concerning the mechanism of evolution.

Charles Darwin was the first person to reach an understanding of the mechanism of evolution. The concept of natural selection that he masterly put forward in *The Origin of Species* in 1859 remains the keystone of the evolutionary process. The principle of natural selection is now firmly established as the main driving force of evolution. However, the Darwinian thesis has been enriched and refined by recent advances in systematics, ecology, cytology, paleontology, and, above all, in genetics. The modern extension of the great work of Gregor Mendel in heredity has had a profound influence on current evolutionary thought. The mechanism of evolution is incomprehensible without familiarity with the fundamentals of genetics. Such basic principles of genetics as are necessary for an understanding of evolution are included in this text.

The opening chapter introduces the student to a specific population of organisms in which a novel trait has suddenly appeared among its members. One of the important considerations immediately imparted to the reader is that evolution is a property of populations. A population is not a mere assemblage of individuals, but a breeding community of individuals. Moreover, it is the *population* that evolves in time, *not* the *individual*. The individual does not evolve, for he survives for only one generation. An individual, however, ensures continuity to a population by leaving offspring. Life is maintained only by the propagation of new individuals, differing in some degree from their parents. It will become apparent that the future success or failure of a population depends to a large extent on the numbers and kinds of offspring produced each generation. A deep appreciation of evolutionary changes in populations requires knowledge of mathematics. The general reader, however, should experience no difficulty with the mathematical considerations in this book, as the treatment is minimal and kept at an elementary level.

The text is simplified by numerous illustrations. The drawings, many of them original, were executed by my wife, Mrs. Carolyn Thorne Volpe. The illustrations do not merely adorn the pages; all are important in supporting the writing. Selected references accompany each chapter in the hope that the student will want to extend his knowledge of evolution beyond that presented here.

The book could not have been prepared without the knowledge derived from my past teachers and students. The latter, perhaps unknowingly, have also been my teachers. If simplicity and clarity of presentation of the subject matter have been achieved in this book, it will be due, in great measure, to the long-suffering college freshmen in my introductory general biology course for some fifteen years. I appreciate the helpful suggestions and advice from several colleagues, particularly Dr. Andrew A. Arata, Dr. David J. Merrell, and Dr. Edward J. Kormondy. I wish also to acknowledge the able assistance of Mrs. Mary Eastin, who cheerfully typed the manuscript in its various forms, and of Mrs. Paula Chane Gebhardt, who worked tirelessly in preparing the Index and in reading proofs. Finally, I am indebted to the authors and publishers who have generously granted permission to use figures and tables from their books. Individual acknowledgments are made where the figures and charts appear in the text.

E. Peter Volpe

New Orleans, Louisiana
1971

1 Meaning of Evolution

In the fall of 1958, the folks of a quiet, rural community in the southern part of the United States were startled and dismayed by the occurrence, in large numbers, of multilegged bullfrogs in an 85-acre artificial lake on a cotton farm. Widespread newspaper publicity of this strange event attracted the attention of university scientists, curiosity seekers, and gourmets. The lake supports a large population of bullfrogs, estimated at several thousands. Although reports tended to be exaggerated, there were undoubtedly in excess of 350 multilegged deviants. As illustrated in Figure 1.1, the extra legs were oddly positioned, but they were unmistakably copies of the two normal hind limbs. Incredibly the extra limbs were functional, but their movements were perceptibly not in harmony with the pair of normal legs. The bizarre multilegged frogs were clumsy and graceless.

All the multilegged frogs appeared to be of the same age, approximately two years old, and of the same generation. These atypic frogs were found only during the one season, and were not detected again in subsequent years. The multilegged frogs disappeared almost as dramatically as they had appeared.

Strange and exceptional events of this kind are of absorbing interest, and challenge us for an explanation. How do such oddities arise and what are the factors responsible for their ultimate disappearance in a natural population? In ancient times, bodily deformities evoked reverential awe and inspired some fanciful tales. Early man constructed a number of myths to explain odd events totally beyond his control or comprehension. One legend has it that when masses of skeletons are revived or reanimated, the bones of different animals often become confused. Another old idea is that grotesquely shaped frogs are throwbacks to some remote prehistoric ancestor. These accounts are, of course, novelistic and illusory. They do, however, reveal the uniquely imaginative capacity of the human mind.

1

MULTILEGGED BULLFROGS

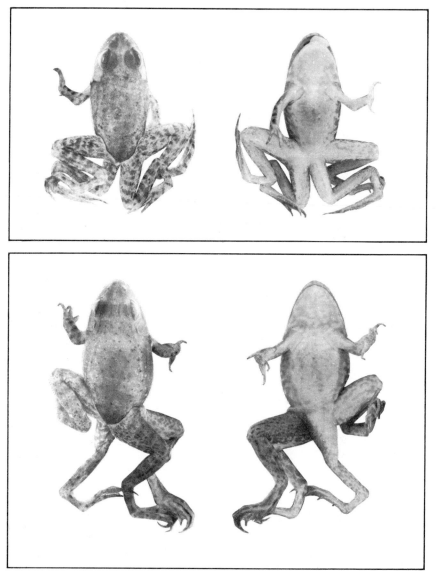

FIG. 1.1. Two multilegged frogs, each viewed from the back (dorsal) and front (ventral) surface. These bizarre bullfrogs were discovered in October, 1958, in a lake near Tunica, Mississippi. Several hundred frogs with extra hind limbs were found at this locality. How does such an abnormality arise? Two reasonable interpretations are set forth in chapter 1.

Nevertheless, we should seek a completely different cause-and-effect sequence, relying more on our faculty for logical analysis.

ENVIRONMENTAL MODIFICATION

Inspection alone cannot reveal the underlying cause of the multi-legged anomaly. We may thoroughly dissect the limbs and describe in detail the anatomy of each component, but no amount of dissection can tell us how the malformation arose. The deformity either was foreordained by heredity or originated from injury to the embryo at a vulnerable stage in its development. We shall direct our attention first to the latter possibility and its implications.

Some external factor in the environment may have adversely affected the pattern of development of the hind limb region. The cotton fields around the pond were periodically sprayed with pesticides to combat noxious insects. It is not inconceivable that the chemicals used were potent *teratogens* —that is, substances capable of causing marked distortions of normal body parts.

That chemical substances can have detrimental effects on the developing organism is well documented. For example, the geneticist Walter Landauer demonstrated in the 1950's that a wide variety of chemicals, such as boric acid, pilocarpine, and insulin (normally a beneficial hormone), can produce abnormalities of the legs and beaks when injected into chick embryos. This type of finding cannot be dismissed complacently as an instance of a laboratory demonstration without parallel in real life. Indeed, in 1961, medical researchers discovered with amazement amounting to incredulity that a purportedly harmless sleeping pill made of the drug thalidomide, when taken by a pregnant woman, particularly during the second month of pregnancy, could lead to a grotesque deformity in the newborn baby, a rare condition in humans called phocomelia—literally, "seal limbs." The arms are absent or reduced to tiny, flipper-like stumps (Fig. 1.2).

In different organisms—fish, frog, mice, and man—anomalies can be caused by such diverse agents as extremes of temperature, X-rays, viruses, drugs, diet deficiencies, and lack of oxygen. More than a century ago, in 1832, the French biologist Etienne Geoffroy-St. Hilaire sealed with varnish the air pores in the shell of a hen's egg, and observed that the embryo, deprived of its oxygen supply, became deformed. Experiments by modern investigators, like Theodore Ingalls of Harvard University, have confirmed St. Hilaire's crude, but informative, experiment. Deprivation of oxygen during the early divisions of fertilized eggs of the zebra fish can lead to the formation of abnormally small eyes or a single eye only. In 1941, the med-

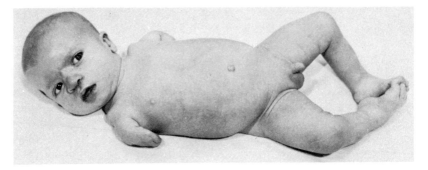

FIG. 1.2. Armless deformity in the newborn infant, resulting from the action of thalidomide, a sedative taken by his mother in her second month of pregnancy. (Courtesy of Dr. W. Lenz.)

ical community was startled by the observation that pregnant women who had contracted German measles during the first three months of pregnancy gave birth to blinded infants. The infants were afflicted with cataract, a condition in which the eye lens are opaque, obstructing the passage of light. There is no longer the slightest doubt that environmental factors may be causal agents of specific defects. A variation that arises as a direct response to some external change in the environment, and not by any change in the genetic makeup of the individual, is referred to as an *environmental modification.*

If the multilegged anomaly in the bullfrog was environmentally induced, we may surmise, as depicted in Figure 1.3, that the harmful chemical or other causative factor acted during the sensitive early embryonic stage. Moreover, if some external agent had brought about the abnormality in the bullfrog, this agent must have been effective only once, as the multilegged condition did not occur repeatedly over the years. It may be that the harmful environmental factor did not recur, in which event we would not expect the malformation to reappear.

Our suppositions could be put to a test by controlled breeding experiments, the importance of which cannot be overstated. Only through breeding tests can the basis of the variation be firmly established. If the anomaly constituted an environmental modification, then, as illustrated in Figure 1.3, a cross of two multilegged bullfrogs would yield all normal progeny. In the absence of any disturbing environmental factors, the offspring would develop normal hind limbs. This breeding experiment was not actually performed, as none of the malformed frogs survived to sexual maturity. Nonetheless, we have brought into focus an important biological principle: *environmentally induced traits cannot be passed on to another generation.*

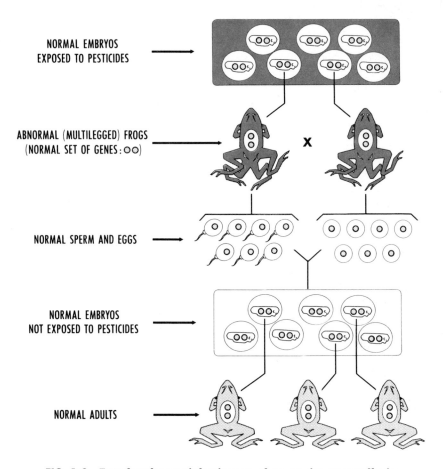

NORMAL EMBRYOS
EXPOSED TO PESTICIDES

ABNORMAL (MULTILEGGED) FROGS
(NORMAL SET OF GENES: oo)

NORMAL SPERM AND EGGS

NORMAL EMBRYOS
NOT EXPOSED TO PESTICIDES

NORMAL ADULTS

FIG. 1.3. Test for the noninheritance of an environmentally induced trait. If the malformation of the hind limbs arose from without by the action of an adverse environmental agent (pesticide) and not from within by genetic change, then the abnormality would *not* be transmitted from parent to offspring. The multilegged parents, although visibly abnormal, are both genetically normal. Normal hind limbs are expected if, during development, the offspring are not exposed to the same injurious environmental agents as were the parents.

The only elements that are transmitted to the next generation are two tiny bits of living matter, the egg and the sperm. These two extraordinary blobs of protoplasm comprise the sole perpetuators of life. The hereditary qualities of the offspring are established at the time the sperm unites with the egg. The basic hereditary determiners, the *genes*, occur in pairs in the fertilized egg. Each inherited characteristic is governed by at least one pair of genes. One member of each pair comes from the male parent and the other from the female parent. Stated another way, the sperm and egg each have half the number of genes of the parents. Fertilization restores the original number and the paired condition (Fig. 1.3).

The underlying assumption in the cross depicted in Figure 1.3 is that the genes which influence the development of the hind limbs are normal. Of course, the multilegged parents themselves possess normal genes. Now it might seem strange that an abnormal character can result from a perfectly sound set of genes. However, normal genes cannot be expected to act normally under all environmental circumstances. A gene may be likened to a photographic negative. A perfect negative (normal gene) may produce an excellent or poor positive print (normal or abnormal trait) depending upon such factors (environmental factors) as the quality or concentration of the chemical solutions used in preparing the print. The environment thus affects the *expression* of the negative (gene), but the negative (gene) itself remains unaffected throughout the making of the print (trait).

We shall learn more about the nature of genes and the mechanism of inheritance in the next chapter. For the moment, the important consideration is that *a given set of genes prescribes a potentiality for a trait, and not the trait itself.* What is inherited is a potential capacity. The potential capacity will not become a developed capacity unless the appropriate environment is furnished. Genes always act within the conditioning framework of the environment.

LAMARCKISM AND LYSENKOISM

Few people would expect bodily deformities caused by harmful environmental factors to be inheritable. And yet, many persons are prone to believe that favorable or beneficial bodily changes acquired or developed during one's lifetime are transmitted to the offspring. As a familiar example, an athlete who exercised and developed large muscles would pass down his powerful muscular development to his children. This is the famous theory of "inheritance of acquired characteristics," or Lamarckism, after Jean Baptiste de Lamarck, the French naturalist of the late 1700's and early 1800's. The concept of Lamarckism has absolutely no foundation of factual evidence. We know, for instance, that blonde children are not guaranteed to brunette women who consistently bleach their hair. Circumcision is still necessary in the newborn male despite a rite which has been practiced for well over 4,000 years. It is sufficient to state that the results of countless laboratory experiments testing the possibility of the inheritance of acquired or environmentally induced traits have been emphatically negative.

It would seem that the untenable Lamarckian theory is of historical interest only. However, the biological world in modern times has witnessed a shocking resurrection of Lamarckism. In the mid-1930's, the unprincipled Russian biologist Trofim Lysenko rose to power in the Soviet Communist Party by militantly advocating the Lamarckian doctrine. Lysenko's promise to transform Soviet agriculture rapidly held great appeal for Stalin and his successor, Khrushchev. As Director of the Institute of Genetics of the Academy of Sciences of the Soviet Union, Lysenko dominated and degraded Soviet research in genetics for more than 25 years. He derided classical genetical principles and purged his scientific opponents, among them being the world-renowned Russian geneticist Nikolai Vavilov. Lysenko sought to improve crop plants by exposing the seeds to a variety of harsh environmental conditions, like extremely high and low temperatures. He boasted that characteristics induced by strong environmental agents became impressed on all future generations. When spring varieties of wheat and barley were exposed to low temperatures, Lysenko claimed that the varieties became "educated" to be winter-resistant plants. His spectacular claims were unfounded, and his ill-based plant breeding program proved ultimately a dismal failure. Lysenko's downfall came in early 1965, following closely the exit of Khrushchev in late 1964. A normal scientific atmosphere has been restored in Soviet genetic research.

The preceding considerations bear significantly on our bullfrog population. We have not been able to perform the critical breeding test to prove or disprove that the multilegged trait is a noninheritable modification. However, let us for the moment accept the thesis that the multilegged condition was environmentally induced and examine the implications of this view in terms of the population as a whole. Outwardly there appears to have been a striking change in the bullfrog population. But, in actuality, since the basic hereditary materials, the genes, have not been affected in any way, the composition of the population has remained essentially unaltered. In other words, there has been no change in the population of evolutionary significance. Evolution can occur *only* where there is inheritable variation.

INHERITABLE VARIATION

We shall now examine the possibility that the multilegged frogs were genetically abnormal. One or more of their genes may have been defective. Unlike teratogens, which damage an already-conceived offspring and affect only a single generation, detrimental genes occur in the germ plasm before conception and may lie dormant for several generations.

We shall postulate that the defective gene for the multilegged condition is *recessive* to the normal gene. That is to say, the expression of the defective gene is completely masked or suppressed by the normal (or dominant) gene when the two are present together in the same individual (Fig. 1.4). Such an individual, normal in appearance but harboring the

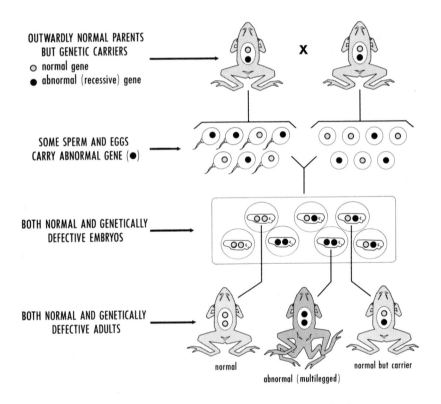

FIG. 1.4. Mating of two "carrier" parents resulting in the emergence of multilegged offspring. The multilegged trait is assumed to be controlled by an abnormal recessive gene. Both parents are normal in appearance, but each carries the abnormal gene masked by the normal gene. The recessive gene manifests its detrimental effect when the offspring inherits one abnormal gene from each of its parents.

harmful recessive gene, is said to be a *carrier*. The recessive gene may be transmitted without any outward manifestation for several generations, continually being sheltered by its dominant partner. However, as seen in Figure 1.4, the detrimental recessive gene ultimately becomes exposed when two carrier parents happen to mate. Those progeny which are endowed with two recessive genes, one from each parent, are malformed. On the average, one fourth of the offspring will be multilegged.

Genetic defects transmitted by recessive genes are not at all unusual. Pertinent to the present discussion is an inherited syndrome of abnormalities in humans, known as the Ellis-van Creveld syndrome. Afflicted individuals are disproportionately dwarfed (short-limbed), have malformed hearts, and possess six fingers on each hand (Fig. 1.5). The recessive gene

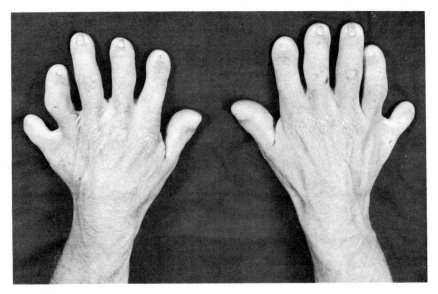

FIG. 1.5. Six-digited hands, one of the manifestations of the Ellis-van Creveld syndrome in humans, a rare recessive deformity. Affected offspring generally come from two normal, but carrier, parents, each of which harbors the abnormal recessive gene. (Courtesy of Dr. Victor A. McKusick.)

that is responsible for this complex of defects is exceedingly rare. Yet, as shown by the geneticist Victor A. McKusick of Johns Hopkins University, the Ellis-van Creveld anomaly occurs with an exceptionally high incidence among the Amish people in Lancaster County, Pennsylvania. The defective recessive gene apparently was present in one member of the original Old Order Amish immigrants from Europe two centuries ago. For a few generations, the detrimental gene was passed down unobserved, masked by its normal partner gene. Since 1860, the Ellis-van Creveld deformity has appeared in at least 50 unfortunate offspring. Ordinarily, it is uncommon for both members of a married couple to harbor the defective recessive gene. However, in the sober religious Amish community, marriages have been largely confined within members of the sect with a resulting high degree of consanguinity. Marriages of close relatives have tended to promote the meeting of two normal, but carrier, parents.

We know very little about the past history or breeding structure of the particular bullfrog population in which the multilegged trait appeared with an exceptionally high frequency. We may suspect that all 350 or more multilegged frogs were derived from a single mating of two carrier parents. In contrast to humans, a single mated pair of frogs can produce well over 10,000 offspring. The similarity in age of the multilegged frogs found in nature adds weight to the supposition that these frogs are members of one generation, and probably of one mating.

Much of the foregoing discussion on the bullfrog is admittedly speculative. However, one aspect is certain: *previously concealed harmful genes are brought to light through the mechanism of heredity.* A trait absent for many generations can suddenly appear without warning. Once a variant character expresses itself, its fate will be determined by the ability of the individual displaying the trait to survive and reproduce in its given environment.

It is difficult to imagine that the grotesquely shaped frogs could compete successfully with their normal kin. However, we shall never know whether or not the multilegged frogs were capable of contending with the severities of climatic or seasonal changes, or of successfully escaping their predators, or even of actively defending themselves. What we do know is that the multilegged frogs did not survive to reproductive age. Despite diligent searches by many interested investigators, no sexually mature abnormal frogs have been uncovered in the natural population. It appears as if this unfavorable variant has been eliminated. Let us now explore this situation in light of Darwin's theory of natural selection.

DARWIN'S NATURAL SELECTION

Slightly more than a century ago, in 1859, Charles Robert Darwin (Fig. 1.6) gave the biological world the master key that unlocked all previous perplexities about evolution. His revolutionary idea of natural selection can be compared only with Newton's law of gravitation and Einstein's theory of relativity. The concept of natural selection was set forth clearly and convincingly by Darwin in his monumental treatise, the *Origin of Species*. This

FIG. 1.6. Charles Darwin at the age of 31 (1840), four years after his famous voyage round the world as an unpaid naturalist aboard H. M. S. *Beagle*. (From a water color by George Richmond; courtesy of the American Museum of Natural History.)

epoch-making book was the fruition of more than 20 years of meticulous accumulation and analysis of facts. The first edition, some 1,500 copies, was sold out on the very day it appeared, November 24, 1859. The book was immediately both acidly attacked and effusively praised. Today, the *Origin of Species* remains the one book to be read by all serious students of nature. The full title of Darwin's treatise was *On the Origin of Species by Means of Natural Selection, or the Preservation of Favoured Races in the Struggle for Life.*

Ironically, Darwin probably would not have prepared his famed volume when he did had not a fellow naturalist in the Dutch East Indies, Alfred Russell Wallace, independently conceived of the idea of natural selection. Wallace's essay and a portion of Darwin's manuscript, each containing remarkably similar views, were read simultaneously before the Linnaean Society in London on July 1, 1858. The joint reading of the papers stirred little interest. Darwin then labored for eight months to compress his voluminous notes into a single book, which he modestly called "only an Abstract." Wallace shares with Darwin the honor of establishing the mechanism by which evolution is brought about, but it was the *Origin of Species*, with its impressive weight of evidence and argument, that left its mark on mankind. The evidence that Darwin marshaled to support his thesis of natural selection was based largely on observations made on his famous voyage round the world on a British Navy ship, H. M. S. *Beagle* (Fig. 1.7).

The doctrine of evolution—that all organisms, including man, are modified descendants of previously existing forms of life—did not originate with Darwin. There were many before him, notably Lamarck, Buffon, and his grandfather, Erasmus Darwin, who recognized or intimated that animals and plants had not remained unchanged through time, but were continuously changing. Indeed, early Greek philosophers, who wondered about everything, speculated on the gradual progression of life from simple to complex. It was reserved for Darwin to remove the doctrine of evolution from the domain of speculation. Darwin's outstanding achievement was his discovery of the principle of natural selection. In showing *how* evolution occurs, Darwin convinced skeptics that evolution *does* occur.

The writings of an English clergyman, Thomas Henry Malthus, provided the germ for Darwin's thesis of natural selection. Malthus, in his famous *An Essay on the Principle of Population*, expressed the realistic view that man's reproductive capacity far exceeds the available food supply. Men compete among themselves for the necessities of life. The unrelenting competition engenders vice, misery, war, and famine. Competition exists among all living things, and it occurred to Darwin that the

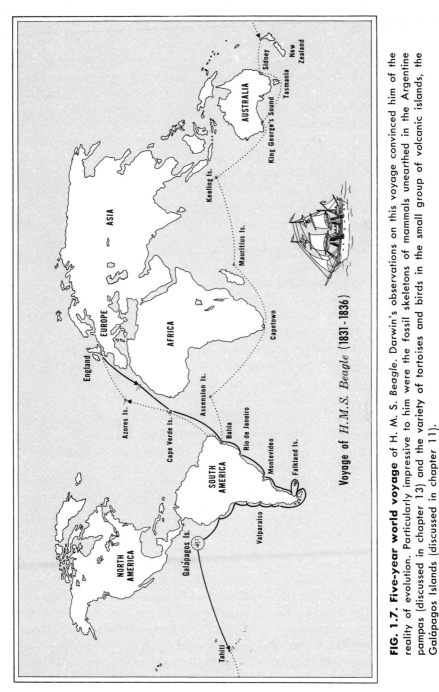

FIG. 1.7. Five-year world voyage of H. M. S. Beagle. Darwin's observations on this voyage convinced him of the reality of evolution. Particularly impressive to him were the fossil skeletons of mammals unearthed in the Argentine pampas (discussed in chapter 13) and the variety of tortoises and birds in the small group of volcanic islands, the Galápagos Islands (discussed in chapter 11).

"struggle for existence" might be the means by which the well-adapted individuals survive and the ill-adjusted are eliminated.

As a whole, the principle of natural selection stems from three important observations and two deductions that logically follow from them. The first observation is that all living things tend to increase their numbers at a prolific rate. A single oyster may produce as many as 100 million eggs at one spawning; one tropical orchid may form well over one million seeds; and a single salmon can deposit 28 million eggs in one season. It is equally apparent (the second observation) that no one group of organisms swarms uncontrollably over the surface of the earth. In fact, the actual size of a given population of any particular organism remains relatively constant over long periods of time. If we accept these readily confirmable observations, the conclusion necessarily follows that not all individuals that are produced in any generation can survive. There is inescapably in nature an intense "struggle for existence."

Darwin's third observation was that individuals in a population are not alike but differ in various features. That all living things vary is indisputable. Those individuals endowed with the most favorable variations, concluded Darwin, would have the best chance of surviving and passing their favorable characteristics on to their progeny. This "survival of the fittest" was termed *natural selection*. (It was the British philosopher Herbert Spencer who proposed the expression "survival of the fittest," which Darwin accepted as equivalent to natural selection. Spencer was a fervent supporter of Darwin's views.)

Darwin presents the essence of his concept of natural selection in the Introduction to the *Origin of Species*, as follows:

As many more individuals of each species are born than can possibly survive; and as, consequently, there is a frequently recurring struggle for existence, it follows that any being, if it vary however slightly in any manner profitable to itself, under the complex and sometimes varying conditions of life, will have a better chance of surviving, and thus be *naturally selected*. From the strong principle of inheritance, any selected variety will tend to propagate its new and modified form.

SURVIVAL OF THE FITTEST

The survival of favorable variants is one facet of the Darwinian concept of natural selection. Equally important is the corollary that unfavorable variants do not survive and multiply. Nature selects against those individuals who are not suited for given conditions of existence. Consequently, natural selection necessarily embraces two aspects, as inseparable as the two faces of the same coin: the negative (elimination of the unfit) and the positive (perpetuation of the fit). In its negative role, natural selection serves as a conservative or stabilizing force, pruning out the aberrant forms from a population.

The superior or fit individuals are popularly extolled as those that emerge victoriously in brutal combat. Fitness has often been naively confused with physical, or even athletic, prowess. This glorification is traceable to such seductive catch phrases as the "struggle for existence" and the "survival of the fittest." What does fitness actually signify?

The true gauge of fitness is not merely survival, but the organism's capacity to leave offspring. An individual must survive in order to reproduce, but not all individuals that survive do, or are able to, leave descendants. We have seen that the multilegged bullfrogs were not successful in propagating themselves. They failed to make a contribution to the next or succeeding generations. They were therefore unfit. Hence, an individual is unfit if he produces no progeny. He is also unfit if he does produce progeny, none of whom survives to maturity. The less spectacular normal-legged frogs did reproduce, and to the extent that they are represented by descendants in subsequent generations, they are the fittest. Fitness, therefore, is measured in terms of reproductive effectiveness. Natural selection can thus be thought of as *differential reproduction,* rather than differential survival.

EVOLUTION DEFINED

Any given generation is descended from only a small fraction of the previous generation. It should be evident that the genes transmitted by those individuals who are most successful in reproduction will predominate in the next generation. As a result of unequal reproductive capacities of individuals having different hereditary constitutions, the genetic characteristics of a population become altered each successive generation. This is a dynamic process which has occurred in the past, occurs today, and will continue to occur as long as there is inheritable variation and differing reproductive abilities. Under these circumstances the composition of a population can never remain constant. This, then, is evolution—*changes in the genetic composition of a population with the passage of each generation.*

The outcome of the evolutionary process is adaptation of the organism to its environment. Many of the structural features of organisms are marvels of construction. It is, however, not at all remarkable that organisms possess particular characteristics that appear to be precisely and peculiarly suited to their needs. This is comprehensible because the individuals that leave the most descendants are more often those that are best equipped to cope with the special environmental conditions to which they are exposed. In other words, the more reproductively fit individuals tend to be those that are better adapted to the environment.

Throughout the ages, appropriate adaptive structures have arisen as the result of gradual changes in the hereditary endowment of a population. Admittedly, events that occurred in the past are not amenable to direct observation or experimental verification. There are no living eye-witnesses of very distant events. The process of evolution in the past has to be inferred. Nevertheless, we may be confident that the same evolutionary forces we witness in operation today have guided evolution in the past. The basis for this confidence is imparted in the chapters ahead.

SUGGESTIONS FOR FURTHER READING

BARNETT, L. and Editorial Staff of *Life*. 1955. *The world we live in*. New York: Time, Inc. Book Division.

CARTER, G. S. 1957. *A hundred years of evolution*. London: Sidgwick & Jackson, Ltd., Publishers.

DARWIN, C. 1958. *The origin of species* (1859). New York: New American Library of World Literature, Inc.

DARWIN, C. 1960. *The voyage of the Beagle* (1840). New York: Bantam Books, Inc.

DEBEER, G. 1964. *Atlas of evolution*. London: Thomas Nelson & Sons.

DOBZHANSKY, T. 1956. *The biological basis of human freedom*. New York: Columbia University Press.

EISELEY, L. 1957. *The immense journey*. New York: Random House, Inc.

GREENE, J. C. 1961. *The death of Adam*. New York: New American Library of World Literature, Inc.

LERNER, I. M. 1968. *Heredity, evolution, and society*. San Francisco: W. H. Freeman & Company, Publishers.

MERRELL, D. J. 1962. *Evolution and genetics*. New York: Holt, Rinehart, and Winston, Inc.

MOODY, P. A. 1962. *Introduction to evolution*. New York: Harper & Row, Publishers.

MOORE, R. and Editors of *Life*. 1964. *Evolution*. New York: Time, Inc. Book Division.

SIMPSON, G. G. 1951. *The meaning of evolution*. New York: New American Library of World Literature, Inc.

WALLACE, B. and SRB, A. M. 1964. *Adaptation*. Englewood Cliffs, N.J.: Prentice-Hall, Inc.

2 Genetic Variation

Darwin recognized that the process of evolution is inseparably linked to the mechanism of inheritance. But he could not satisfactorily explain how a given trait is passed down from parent to offspring, nor could he adequately account for the sudden appearance of new traits. Unfortunately, Darwin was unaware of the great discovery in heredity made by a contemporary, the humble Austrian monk Gregor Johann Mendel.

Mendel's manuscript appeared in print in 1866. His published paper was overlooked by most scientists of the day, including Darwin. The distinguished German botanist Karl von Nägeli is known to have corresponded with Mendel, but he surprisingly failed to grasp that Mendel had formulated the fundamental laws of inheritance. Mendel's important contribution lay ignored or unknown until 1900, sixteen years after his death. The rediscovery of Mendel's publication at the beginning of the century ushered in the science of genetics and ultimately led to our current understanding of variation.

MENDEL'S LAW OF SEGREGATION

Mendel's historic study on the common garden pea in a small monastery garden is now a familiar story. He obtained from seedsmen numerous purebred varieties of peas, which differed in such characteristics as vine height, position of the flowers, shape and color of the seeds, and configuration of the pods. He painstakingly grew each variety for two years to establish beyond doubt that each bred true to type. Pea plants are normally self-fertilizing. However, artificial cross-fertilizations can be readily accomplished by removing the pollen-producing organs (stamens) of the flower bud, and subsequently transferring pollen (containing the male sex cell, or sperm) from another flower to the egg-producing organ (pistil).

17

The simplest of Mendel's experiments is shown in Figure 2.1. A pure-bred variety of tall plants (about 6 feet in height) was artificially crossed with a purebred short form (1 foot high). When seeds of this cross were grown, the plants that emerged were not intermediate in height but all resembled one of the parents. The whole of this first filial (F_1) generation consisted solely of tall plants. Mendel termed the condition of tallness the *dominant* characteristic, and the short condition, which did not appear among the F_1 progeny, the *recessive* characteristic. The F_1 plants were allowed to self-fertilize, and the second filial (F_2) generation was found to contain both tall and short plants. Actual counts showed that 75 percent of the F_2 offspring were tall and 25 percent were short. In comparable crosses involving other pairs of traits, Mendel observed that the recessive characteristic, which seemingly disappeared in the first generation, invari-ably reappeared to make up a quarter of the second generation.

Mendel concluded that there must be discrete material units, or fac-tors, which control inheritance. He envisioned each trait as being deter-mined by a pair of factors, now known as *genes*. The genes comprising a given pair may be alike or may be different. If the members are contrasting, one (the dominant gene) typically masks the expression of its partner (the recessive gene). The dominant gene is customarily symbolized by a capital letter (e.g., T); the recessive gene, by a corresponding small letter (t). A purebred tall plant is said to be *homozygous* for tallness (TT). It may be also referred to as a dominant homozygote. A plant that is genet-ically *tt* is homozygous for shortness or, as we often say, is a recessive homozygote. The F_1 offspring illustrated in the cross in Figure 2.1 is a heterozygote; in other words, it is *heterozygous* for tallness, carrying two unlike genes (Tt).

If the genes occur in pairs in an individual, then evidently some process must take place to ensure that each gamete (egg or sperm) contains one, and only one, member of a pair of genes. Mendel had no knowledge of the special kind of nuclear division (meiosis) that occurs during the produc-tion of the sex cells. However, he correctly inferred that the members of a pair of genes must separate, or segregate, from each other during gamete formation. Thus, a given gamete can carry T or t, but not both. This funda-mental concept that only one member of any pair of genes in a parent is transmitted to each offspring is Mendel's first law, known as the *Law of Segregation.*

Figure 2.1 shows that the F_1 heterozygote (Tt) produces two kinds of pollen cells (sperm); half the pollen carry the T gene and the other half carry the t gene. The same two kinds occur in equal proportions among the egg cells. Each kind of pollen has an equal chance of meeting each kind of egg. The random meeting of gametes leads to the formation of three

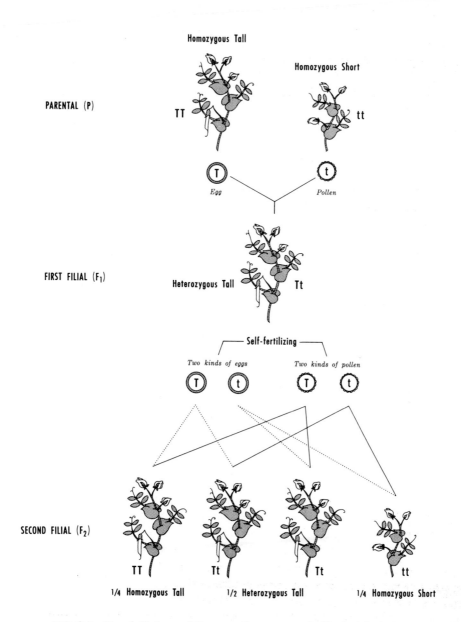

PARENTAL (P)

Homozygous Tall

TT

Homozygous Short

tt

T
Egg

t
Pollen

FIRST FILIAL (F₁)

Heterozygous Tall   Tt

Self-fertilizing

Two kinds of eggs   *Two kinds of pollen*

T   t   T   t

SECOND FILIAL (F₂)

TT   Tt   Tt   tt

1/4 Homozygous Tall   1/2 Heterozygous Tall   1/4 Homozygous Short

FIG. 2.1. Mendel's Law of Segregation, as revealed in the inheritance of vine height (tall vs. short) in the pea plant.

genetically different types of individuals, or technically, three different *genotypes: TT, Tt*, and *tt*. The ratio of genotypes in the F_2 generation may be expressed as ¼ *TT* : ½ *Tt* : ¼ *tt*, or 0.25 *TT* : 0.50 *Tt* : 0.25 *tt*, or simply 1 *TT* : 2 *Tt* : 1 *tt*. The dominant homozygote (*TT*) cannot be distinguished by inspection from the heterozygote (*Tt*). In genetical parlance, we say that the *TT* and *Tt* genotypes have the same *phenotype* (same external or observable appearance). Thus, on the basis of phenotype alone, the F_2 ratio is ¾ tall : ¼ short, or 0.75 tall : 0.25 short, or finally, 3 tall : 1 short.

Our interpretation of the mode of inheritance of the multilegged trait in the bullfrog was based on the above simple foundation provided by Mendel. In the preceding chapter, we postulated a cross between two normal, but heterozygous, frogs (*Aa*). These phenotypically normal parents, each harboring the abnormal recessive gene, were called carriers, an acceptable descriptive expression but not as precise as the term heterozygotes. The expectation for multilegged offspring (*aa*) from two heterozygous parents is 25 percent, in keeping with Mendel's 3:1 ratio. This cross, using appropriate genetic symbols, is depicted in Figure 2.2.

It should be understood that the 3:1 phenotypic ratio is an expectation based on probability. The production of large numbers of offspring increases the probability of obtaining a 3:1 ratio, just as many tosses of a coin improve the chances of approximating the expected 1 "head" : 1 "tail" ratio. If a coin is tossed only two times, a "head" on the first toss is not invariably followed by a "tail" on the second toss. In like manner, if only four offspring are produced by two heterozygous parents, it should not be thought that three dominant phenotypes will be invariably accompanied by one recessive phenotype. With small numbers of progeny, as is characteristic in man, any ratio might arise in a given family. Nonetheless, the Mendelian ratios enable us to predict the probability of an event. For example, albinism (lack of pigmentation) in man is the result of a recessive gene in the homozygous state (*cc*). When the parents are both heterozygous carriers (*Cc*), the chance of this normal couple having an albino child is one out of four. If the first child is an albino, the probability of albinism in the second or any subsequent child remains the same (25 percent), as each birth is an entirely independent event.

MENDEL'S LAW OF INDEPENDENT ASSORTMENT

Mendel also established the *Law of Independent Assortment*, which states that one trait (one gene pair) segregates independently of another trait (another gene pair). This principle stemmed from the outcome of crosses of two pea plants that differed from each other in two characteristics. As seen in Figure 2.3, a variety characterized by yellow and round

NORMAL (Heterozygous) PARENTS

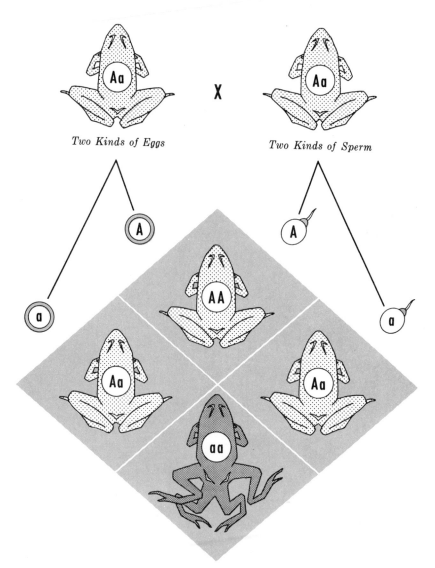

3/4 NORMAL : 1/4 MULTILEGGED

FIG. 2.2. Cross of two heterozygous carrier frogs. One quarter of the offspring are normal and completely devoid of the recessive gene (AA); one half are normal but carriers, like the parents (Aa); and the remaining one quarter exhibit the multilegged anomaly (aa).

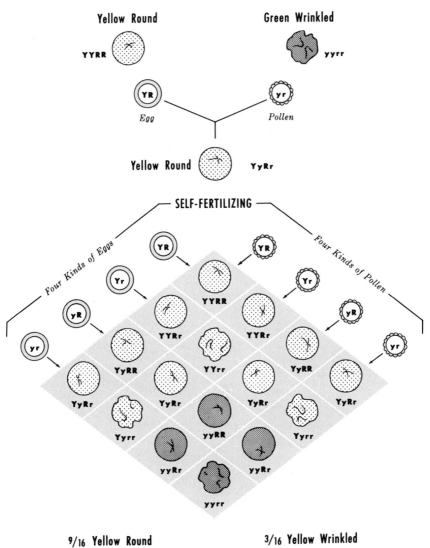

9/16 Yellow Round   3/16 Yellow Wrinkled

3/16 Green Round   1/16 Green Wrinkled

FIG. 2.3. Mendel's Law of Independent Assortment, as revealed in the inheritance of two pairs of characters (color and shape of the seed) in the pea plant.

seeds (*YYRR*) was crossed with a variety in which the seeds were green and wrinkled (*yyrr*). Only the dominant characteristics (yellow, round) were displayed by the F_1 plants (*YyRr*). In contrast to the uniformity in the F_1 generation, four different phenotypes arose in the F_2 generation, two like the original parents and two new combinations (yellow, wrinkled and green, round). The four F_2 phenotypes appeared in a ratio of 9:3:3:1. For such a ratio to be obtained, the F_1 plants (*YyRr*) must have produced four kinds of gametes in equal proportions: *YR*, *Yr*, *yR*, and *yr*. Stated another way, the segregation of the members of one pair of genes must have occurred independently of the segregation of the members of the other gene pair during gamete formation. Thus, 50 percent of the gametes received *Y*, and of these same gametes, half obtained *R* and the other half *r*. Accordingly, 25 percent of the gametes were *YR* and 25 percent were *Yr*. Likewise, 50 percent of the gametes carried *y*, of which half contained as well *R* and half *r* (or 25 percent *yR* and 25 percent *yr*). The four kinds of egg cells and the four kinds of pollen (sperm) can unite in 16 possible ways, as shown graphically in the F_2 "checkerboard" in Figure 2.3.

The convenient checkerboard method of analysis was devised by the British geneticist R. C. Punnett. The eggs and sperm are listed separately on two different sides of the checkerboard, and each square represents an offspring that arises from the union of a given egg cell and a given sperm cell. The "reading" of the squares discloses the classical Mendelian phenotypic ratio of 9:3:3:1 for two pairs of independently assorting genes.

GENETIC RECOMBINATION

The Mendelian principles permit a genuine appreciation of the source of genetic variation in natural populations of organisms. An impressively large array of different kinds of individuals can arise from the simple processes of segregation and recombination of genes that automatically take place in sexually reproducing organisms. To document this point, let us consider a few of the independently assorting traits in the fruit fly, *Drosophila melanogaster*. This small insect, approximately one fourth the size of a house fly, has long been a favorite subject for genetical research. Numerous variations have been found, affecting all parts of the body. The pair of wings may be reduced in length to small vestiges, the result of the action of a recessive gene, termed vestigial (Fig. 2.4). Two heterozygous normal-winged flies, each harboring the gene for vestigial wings, can produce two types of offspring: normal winged and vestigial winged. Now suppose that these same parents have a second concealed recessive gene, which, when homozygous, modifies the normal gray color of the body to black or ebony. Normal-winged, gray-bodied parents can give rise to

| PARENTS | OFFSPRING | FORMULA |

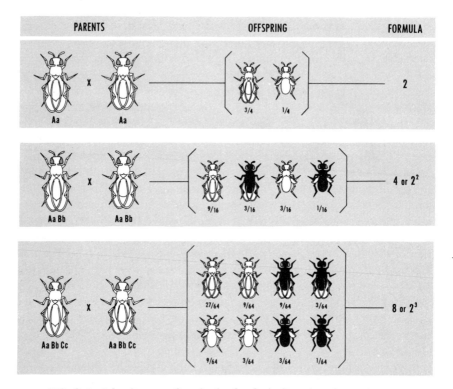

FIG. 2.4. Inheritance of traits in the fruit fly, when the parents are each heterozygous for one (Aa), two (AaBb), and three (AaBbCc) independently assorting traits. The gene for long wings (A) is dominant over the gene for vestigial wings (a); gray body (B) is dominant over ebony (b); normal eyes (C) is dominant over the eyeless condition (c). The number of visibly different classes (phenotypes) of offspring increases progressively with each additional pair of traits. The generalized formula for determining the number of different phenotypes among the offspring (when dominance is complete) is 2^n, where n stands for the number of different heterozygous pairs of genes.

four types of offspring, as illustrated in Figure 2.4. When the parents are each heterozygous for three pairs of independent characters, eight different kinds of offspring are possible. Accordingly, the number of visibly different classes (phenotypes) of offspring is doubled by each additional heterozygous pair of independently assorting genes. If the parents are each heterozygous for ten pairs of genes, the number of different types among the progeny becomes 2^{10}, or 1,024. We need only reflect momentarily on the fact that there are approximately 10,000 pairs of genes in the fruit fly and at least as many in man. The amount of diversity in a population is potentially so great as to be scarcely imaginable. Moreover, our calculations must be treated as underestimates, since the number of theoretically possible gene recombinations is increased by such factors as multiple allelism.

MULTIPLE ALLELES

We have considered up to this point such pairs of contrasting genes as T (tall) and t (short) in the pea plant and A (normal wings) and a (vestigial wings) in the fruit fly. The alternative forms of a given gene are termed *alleles*. Thus, T is an allele of t or, we may also say, T is allelic to t. Now, a gene may exist in more than two forms. Several contrasting forms of a given gene are referred to as *multiple alleles*.

Multiple allelic inheritance is exemplified by the four familiar major blood groups in humans—A, B, AB, and O. A person's blood group is determined by the particular protein molecules (antigens) on the surface of the red cells. In the early 1900's the Austrian scientist Karl Landsteiner discovered that there were two major antigens, A and B. An individual might possess one or the other antigen, in which case he would be either type A or type B, or contain both antigens (type AB), or have neither antigen (type O). There are two corresponding antibodies in the serum of the blood, anti-A and anti-B.

A person does not have the antibody that is capable of destroying his own red cells (Table 2.1). He may, however, have the antibody which

TABLE 2.1   *ABO Blood Groups in Man*

Group	Genotype	Antigens in Cells	Antibodies in Serum	Can Donate Blood to:	Can Receive Blood from:
A	$I^A I^A$ or $I^A i$	A	anti-B	A, AB	A, O
B	$I^B I^B$ or $I^B i$	B	anti-A	B, AB	B, O
AB	$I^A I^B$	A & B	none	AB	A, B, AB, O
O	ii	none	anti-A & anti-B	A, B, AB, O	O

reacts against the antigen possessed by another person. For example, type A individuals lack anti-A but contain the antibody against B. This knowledge provides the basis for the successful transfusion of blood between individuals. The cardinal rule is to avoid introducing antigens that can be destroyed (or agglutinated) by antibodies in the serum of the recipient. Type O persons are the acknowledged "universal donors" since they contain no antigens that could be acted upon by the recipient's antibodies. Type AB persons lack both antibodies and accordingly can receive blood from persons of all types without fear of destroying the cells contributed by the donor.

The mode of inheritance of the blood groups has been deduced from an analysis of large numbers of human pedigrees. Representative marriages are shown in Figure 2.5. When both parents are AB, three types are possible among the offspring: A, B, and AB (cross "1" in Fig. 2.5). Type O children do not arise from such marriages, and the AB offspring arise twice as often as either the A or B sib. Both parents are heterozygous, each containing an allele (designated I^A) responsible for the production of antigen A as well as an allele (I^B) responsible for antigen B. Both alleles are denoted by capital letters, since neither one is dominant to the other and both express themselves in the heterozygote.

Cross "2" in Figure 2.5 reveals that type O parents have only O children. This suggests that the parents and their offspring are homozygous for a recessive gene (designated i). The relation between the three alleles (I^A, I^B, and i) becomes clear from the analysis of AB $\times$ O marriages (cross "3", Fig. 2.5). Children from such marriages are either A or B, in equal proportions, and never O. Thus, genes I^A and I^B, although exhibiting no dominance with respect to each other, are each dominant to allele i. The recessive i gene is incapable of producing an antigen (Table 2.1).

The outcome of an A $\times$ O marriage depends on whether the A parent is homozygous or heterozygous (crosses "4" and "5", Fig. 2.5). If homozygous ($I^A I^A$), only A children are possible; if heterozygous ($I^A i$), both A and O children can be produced. Likewise, as seen in cross "6" (Fig. 2.5), type O children can arise from a B $\times$ O marriage only when the B parent is heterozygous ($I^B i$).

The frequencies of the blood group alleles vary widely in different human populations throughout the world, an intriguing story that we shall discuss in a subsequent chapter. Our immediate interest is the increased genetic variability due to multiple allelism. Six genotypes are possible with three alleles as compared to three genotypes with two alleles. A series of four multiple alleles would yield 10 possible genotypes. If an organism has only 100 genes, each existing in four alternative forms, the total number of different genotypes would be 10^{100}, or 1 followed by 100 zeroes! With even larger numbers of alternative forms of a given gene—as many as 30 are known in some multiple allelic series—the possible varieties of genotypes become almost incomputable.

Evidently, then, the mechanism of inheritance in sexually reproducing organisms permits an endless variety of combinations of genes generation after generation. In fact, the number of gene combinations that may arise is so immense that no single genetic constitution is ever likely to be exactly duplicated in a person (save in identical twins). Each individual is genetically unique.

The twin processes of segregation and recombination of genes may be

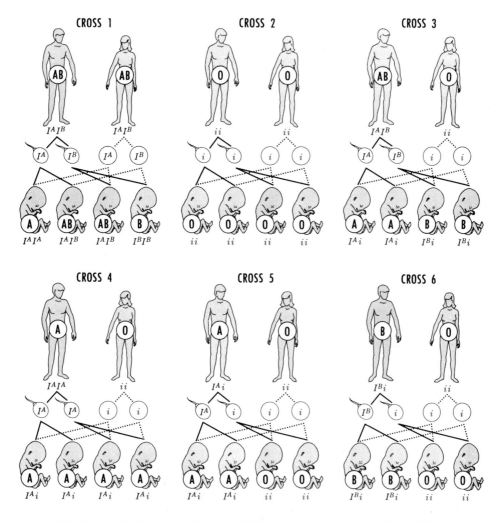

FIG. 2.5. Inheritance pattern of ABO blood groups in man. Three different genes are involved (I^A, I^B, and i), but a given person can possess only two of the genes.

compared, on a very modest scale, to the shuffling and dealing of playing cards. One pack of 52 cards can yield a variety of hands. And, just as in poker where a full house is far superior to three of a kind, so it is in organisms where certain combinations of genes are more advantageous than others. *Only the more beneficial gene combinations are favored by natural selection.*

SUGGESTIONS FOR FURTHER READING

AUERBACH, C. 1961. *The science of genetics.* New York: Harper & Row, Publishers.

BEADLE, G. W. and BEADLE, M. 1968. *The language of life.* Garden City, N.Y.: Doubleday & Co., Inc.

CARSON, H. L. 1963. *Heredity and human life.* New York: Columbia University Press.

KALMUS, H. 1964. *Genetics.* Garden City, N.Y.: Doubleday & Co., Inc.

KOLLER, P. C. 1968. *Chromosomes and genes.* Edinburgh: Oliver & Boyd.

LEVINE, R. P. 1968. *Genetics.* New York: Holt, Rinehart and Winston, Inc.

McKUSICK, V. A. 1969. *Human genetics.* Englewood Cliffs, N.J.: Prentice-Hall, Inc.

SCHEINFELD, A. 1965. *Your heredity and environment.* Philadelphia: J. B. Lippincott Co.

SONNEBORN, T. M. (ed.) 1965. *The control of human heredity and evolution.* New York: The Macmillan Co.

3 Mutation

Each gene of an organism may assume a variety of forms. A normal gene may change to another form, which produces an effect on a trait different from that of the original gene. An inheritable change in the structure of the gene is known as a *mutation*. The variant traits earlier considered— short vine height in the pea plant, vestigial wings in the fruit fly, and albinism in man—all stemmed from the action of altered, or mutant, genes. Mutations, therefore, are the ultimate source of genetic variation. *All differences in the genes of organisms have their origin in mutation.*

CAUSES OF MUTATION

New mutations arise from time to time, and the same mutation may occur repeatedly. It is often quite difficult to distinguish between new mutations and old ones that had occurred previously and had been carried concealed in ancestors. As we have seen, a recessive mutant gene may remain masked by its normal dominant allele for many generations, and reveal itself for the first time only when two heterozygous carriers of the same mutant gene happen to mate.

Each gene runs the risk of changing to an alternative form. The causes of naturally occurring, or "spontaneous," mutations are largely unknown. The environment contains a background of inescapable radiation from radioactive elements, cosmic rays, and gamma rays. It is generally conceded that the amount of background radiation is too low to account for all spontaneous mutations. In other words, only a small fraction of spontaneous mutations can be attributed to background radiation.

In 1927, the late Nobel laureate Hermann J. Muller of Indiana University announced that genes are highly susceptible to the action of X-rays. By irradiating fruit flies with X-rays, he demonstrated that the process of mutation is enormously speeded up. The production of mutations is dependent on the total dosage of X-rays (measured in units called *roent-gens*). Low intensities of X-rays over long periods of time produce as many mutations as the same dose administered in high intensities in a short period of time.

At the time of Muller's discovery, no one conceived that within a generation the entire population of man would be exposed to a significant increase of high-energy radiation as a consequence of the creation of the atomic bomb. The additional amount of high-energy radiation already produced by fallout from atomic explosions has undoubtedly served to increase the mutation rate. Most of the radiation-induced mutations are recessive and most of them are deleterious.

The incidence of malformed infants born to women who had been pregnant at the time of the atomic blasts at Hiroshima and Nagasaki does not appear to have increased above the level found in populations that were not exposed. However, most of the recessive mutations which may have been induced will not be expressed for several generations. Notwithstanding the absence of a demonstrable increase in defects at birth, there is incontrovertible evidence that the sex ratio of the newborns has been altered. If fatal, or lethal, mutations are induced on the X chromosome, they will be immediately expressed in the sons of the woman (Fig. 3.1).

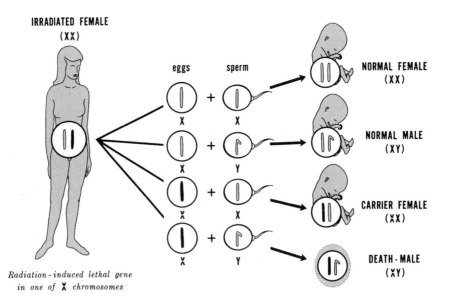

FIG. 3.1. Death of male fetuses resulting from radiation-induced lethal mutations in one of the X chromosomes of the mother.

Deaths of male fetuses prior to birth can be indirectly measured by a decrease in the number of males born to irradiated mothers. Studies on the offspring of Japanese mothers who received a heavy dose of radiation have revealed a significant reduction of male births. Thus, the atomic explosions in Japan are continuing to take their lethal toll.

American and British geneticists estimate that each person currently receives a total dose of 7.8 roentgens to the reproductive cells during the first 30 years of life. Of this amount, 3.1 roentgens are derived from natural background radiation, 4.6 roentgens from various medical uses of ionizing radiation, and an additional 0.1 roentgens from weapons-testing programs already in progress. The additional amount of radiation (0.1 roentgens) received from fallout may seem trivial. However, the exposure of our population to 0.1 roentgens is calculated to induce sufficient mutations to result in 3,750 defective offspring among 100 million births.

CHEMICAL NATURE OF MUTATION

It is now universally accepted that deoxyribonucleic acid (DNA) is the basic chemical component of the gene. The unveiling of the architecture of the DNA molecule, and its recognition as the chemically active portion of the gene, constitute one of the finest triumphs of modern science.

The two scientists who had worked together in the early 1950's to solve the riddle of DNA were Francis H. C. Crick, the young biophysicist at Cambridge University, and James D. Watson, an American student of virology who was then in attendance at Cambridge on a postdoctoral fellowship to study chemistry. With the invaluable aid of X-ray pictures of DNA crystals prepared by Maurice H. F. Wilkins, the biophysicist at King's College in London, Watson and Crick built an inspired model in metal of DNA's configuration. This achievement won Watson, Crick, and Wilkins the coveted Nobel Prize for Medicine and Physiology in 1962.

A remarkable feature of DNA is its simplicity. The DNA molecule is shaped like a twisted ladder (Fig. 3.2). The two parallel strands of the ladder are twisted around each other somewhat like the supporting frameworks of a spiral staircase. The twisted supports of the ladder are made up of phosphate and sugar compounds, while the cross-links or rungs are composed of specific nitrogen-containing ring compounds, or nitrogenous bases. There are two classes of nitrogenous bases, the purines and the pyrimidines. Each rung or step consists of one purine coupled to one pyrimidine. The purine called adenine (A) is normally joined with the pyrimidine called thymine (T) to form what may be termed a "base-pair" step. Another purine, guanine (G), is typically linked with the pyrimidine cytosine (C) to form another base-pair step. These two types of paired bases (A-T and G-C) are arranged in certain sequences, and each gene owes its unique character to a specific order or arrangement of the base-pair steps. A single gene is a linear sequence of at least a thousand bases.

A mutation can be envisioned as a chance mishap to one of the paired bases in the DNA molecule. A single substitution of a C-G pair for a T-A may be sufficient to alter the character of the gene. One possible way in which such a substitution might occur is shown in Figure 3.2. One member of a base-pair (*e.g.*, adenine) may become chemically altered

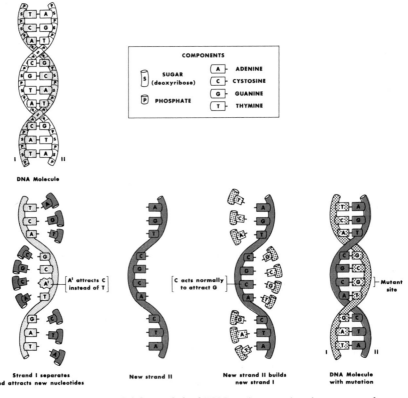

FIG. 3.2. Watson-Crick model of DNA and a postulated sequence of molecular events leading to a mutation. When cell division occurs, the two twisted strands separate and each strand attracts unbound nucleotides (containing nitrogenous compounds, or bases) to rebuild the DNA molecule. The nitrogenous bases are adenine (A), thymine (T), cytosine (C), and guanine (G). This particular illustration shows events through two successive cell divisions, commencing with strand I in the original DNA molecule. During the first division, an adenine radical (A) undergoes a chemical change to A′, which misattracts cytosine (C) instead of thymine (T). At the next division, cytosine (C) attracts its customary partner, guanine (G). The net result is that the granddaughter DNA molecule contains a C-G pair where a T-A pair was formerly located. This highly localized change in one of the pairs of nitrogenous bases may qualify as a gene mutation.

and attract the wrong partner (cytosine instead of thymine). At the next replication of the strand, the misattracted cytosine acts normally to join with guanine. Hence, a C-G pair is established where a T-A pair was formerly located. At this point in the DNA molecule, the gene is modified and may be expected to produce a mutant effect.

The mutation process is generally thought to be an uncontrollable chance phenomenon. Yet the phenomenal surge of knowledge today promises to provide unprecedented opportunities in the future for man to manipulate the DNA molecule in organisms, including himself. The DNA molecule has already been synthesized artificially in the laboratory. The test tube synthesis of a faithful copy of the DNA of a virus was achieved in 1968 by Nobel laureate Arthur Kornberg of Stanford University. Then, in 1969, a team of Harvard researchers, led by Jonathan Beckwith, succeeded in isolating for the first time pure genes of living matter. A single gene (of many bases) was isolated from a virus. These remarkable feats bring closer the day that a hereditary defect in man may be averted by artificially inducing the abnormal gene to "back-mutate" to its normal form.

FREQUENCY OF MUTATIONS

The rate at which any single gene mutates is generally low, but constant. The average rate of mutation per gene in the fruit fly, *Drosophila melanogaster*, is thought to be about 1 in 100,000 gametes. In other words, any given gene, on the average, mutates approximately once in every 100,000 sperm cells or egg cells produced. Some genes change more often than others. In humans, a form of dwarfism known as achondroplasia (or chondrodystrophy) occurs in 1 child in nearly 12,000 born to normal parents. Affected infants are small and disproportionate, with abnormally short arms and legs (Fig. 3.3). The defect is present at birth, and most achondroplastic dwarfs are stillborn or die in infancy. This well-known abnormality is caused by a dominant mutant gene. Since the parents are normal, each new case of this dominant trait must result from a newly mutated gene originating in either the sperm or the egg cell. Twelve thousand births represent a total contribution of 24,000 gametes. Accordingly, a new mutation for this peculiar type of dwarfism arises at a rate of 1 in 24,000 gametes, or roughly 4 in 100,000 gametes (4×10^{-5}).

As another example, we may consider the deleterious dominant gene which results in the formation of malignant tumors in the eye (retinoblastoma). Children afflicted with this dominant disorder die in infancy unless operated upon or treated by radiotherapy. Approximately 50 infants out of one million births are newly affected with retinoblastoma. Therefore, the mutation rate for this dominant gene would be 2.5 in 100,000 gametes (2.5×10^{-5}).

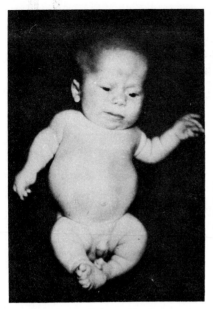

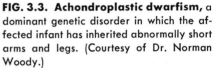

FIG. 3.3. Achondroplastic dwarfism, a dominant genetic disorder in which the affected infant has inherited abnormally short arms and legs. (Courtesy of Dr. Norman Woody.)

Special interest is attached to hemophilia because of its frequent appearance among members of the royal families of Europe since the nineteenth century. The condition, often called "bleeder's disease," is a disorder of the blood in which a vital clotting factor is lacking, causing abnormally delayed clotting. The defect is governed by a recessive mutant gene carried in one of the sex chromosomes, the X chromosome. There is no corresponding gene in the other sex chromosome, the Y. The normal gene shelters the hemophilic gene when present in the female, who contains two X's. Hemophilia is immediately expressed in the male (XY) when he receives the defective gene from his carrier mother. It has been estimated that 3 out of 100,000 gametes bearing X chromosomes contain a newly mutated gene for hemophilia.

The males afflicted with hemophilia in the royal families of Europe trace their ancestry to Queen Victoria of England (Fig. 3.4). Queen Victoria was the original carrier of the fateful gene. Since none of her forebears or relatives was afflicted, the gene for hemophilia apparently originated by mutation in Victoria herself or in a gamete contributed by one of her parents. One of Victoria's four sons suffered from hemophilia and two of her five daughters proved to be carriers of the gene. Through her two carrier daughters, Alice and Beatrice, hemophilia was carried into the Russian and Spanish ruling families. The last Czarevitch of Russia, Alexis, and the two sons of Alfonso XIII, the last king of Spain, were afflicted with hemophilia. Fortunately, the devastating gene has not been carried into

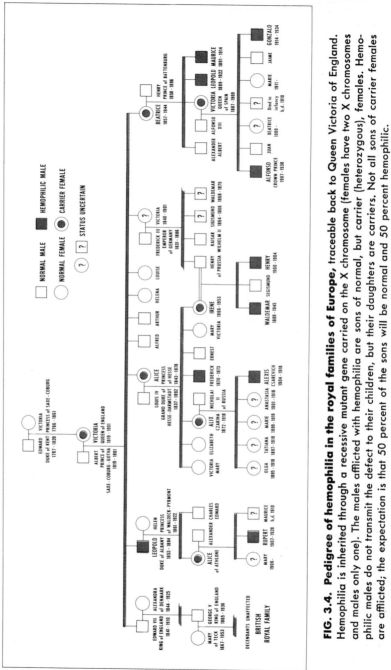

FIG. 3.4. **Pedigree of hemophilia in the royal families of Europe,** traceable back to Queen Victoria of England. Hemophilia is inherited through a recessive mutant gene carried on the X chromosome (females have two X chromosomes and males only one). The males afflicted with hemophilia are sons of normal, but carrier (heterozygous), females. Hemophilic males do not transmit the defect to their children, but their daughters are carriers. Not all sons of carrier females are afflicted; the expectation is that 50 percent of the sons will be normal and 50 percent hemophilic.

the present British royal family. Queen Victoria's eldest son, King Edward VII, was not hemophilic and could not have transmitted the disease to any of his descendants.

THE OVER-ALL MUTATION RATE

Although the mutation rate of a single gene may be low, the mutability of the organism as a whole is obviously much higher when we take into account the total complement of genes possessed by an individual. The total number of genes in the human is at least 25,000. The average rate of mutation per gene in man is generally held to be about 1 or 2 per 100,000 gametes. If the value of 2/100,000 mutations per gene (2×10^{-5}) is selected and multiplied by the conservative figure of 25,000 genes (2.5×10^4), then the average number of new mutations per gamete is 0.50. Thus, one of every two gametes produced by a person would bear a new mutant gene.

Each offspring, of course, is the product of two gametes. Let us envision the random union of sperm cells and egg cells to form zygotes, and adopt the aforementioned figure that 50 percent of all gametes bear one newly mutated gene. The chance that an egg cell containing a newly mutated gene would be fertilized by a sperm cell carrying a new mutant gene is 1 in 4, or 25 percent. (Recall that the probability of both coins falling heads when tossed together is $\frac{1}{2} \times \frac{1}{2} = \frac{1}{4}$.) The chance that a zygote would be free of a newly mutated gene is also 25 percent (like the probability of two tails). Finally, the chance that a zygote would carry a new mutant gene contributed by either the sperm cell or the egg cell is 50 percent (similar to the probability of the combination of a head and a tail when two coins are tossed together). It should be apparent that 75 percent of all human offspring would contain at least one newly mutated gene. Viewed in this manner, the phenomenon of mutation should become very real to us.

HARMFUL NATURE OF MUTATIONS

The vast majority of gene mutations observable today in organisms are changes for the worse. This is not unexpected. Existing populations of organisms are products of a long evolutionary past. The genes that are now normal to the members of a population represent the most favorable mutations selectively accumulated over eons of time. The chance that a new mutant gene will be more advantageous than an already established favorable gene is slim. Nonetheless, if the environment were to change, the previously adverse mutant gene might prove to be beneficial in the new environmental situation. The microscopic water flea, *Daphnia,* thrives at a temperature of 20°C and cannot survive when the temperature rises to 27°C. A mutant strain of this water flea is known which requires temperatures between 25°C and 30°C and cannot live at 20°C. Thus, at high temperatures, the mutant gene is essential to the survival of the water fleas. This little episode reveals an important point: *a mutation that is inferior in the environment in which it arose may be superior in another environment.*

Ideally, mutations should arise only when advantageous, and only when needed. This, of course, is fanciful thinking. Mutations occur irrespective of their usefulness or uselessness. The mutation responsible for the multilegged abnormality in the bullfrog is certainly not beneficial. But novel inheritable characters repeatedly arise as a consequence of mutation. Only one mutation in several thousands might be advantageous, but this one mutation might be important, if not necessary, to the continued success of a population. The harsh price of evolutionary progress is the continual occurrence and elimination of mutant genes with detrimental effects.

SUGGESTIONS FOR FURTHER READING

ASIMOV, I. 1962. *The genetic code.* New York: New American Library of World Literature, Inc.

EMERY, A. E. H. 1968. *Heredity, disease, and man.* Berkeley and Los Angeles: University of California Press.

MACALPINE, I. and HUNTER, R. 1969. Porphyria and King George III. *Scientific American,* July, pp. 38–46.

MOORE, J. A. 1963. *Heredity and development.* New York: Oxford University.

MONTAGU, A. 1963. *Human heredity.* New York: New American Library of World Literature, Inc.

WALLACE, B. 1966. *Chromosomes, giant molecules, and evolution.* New York: W. W. Norton & Co., Inc.

WATSON, J. D. 1965. *Molecular biology of the gene.* New York: W. A. Benjamin, Inc.

WATSON, J. D. 1968. *The double helix.* New York: Atheneum.

4 Genetic Equilibrium

The opening chapter introduced us to a natural population of bull-frogs which conspicuously housed at one time several hundred multilegged variants. We surmised that the multilegged anomaly was an inherited condition, transmitted by a harmful recessive gene. The multilegged frogs disappeared in nature as dramatically as they appeared. They unquestionably failed to reproduce and leave descendants. Now, let us imagine that the multilegged frogs were as reproductively fit as their normal kin. Would the multilegged trait eventually still be eliminated from the population?

A comparable question was posed to the English geneticist R. C. Punnett at the turn of the century. He was asked to explain the prevalence of blue eyes in man in view of the acknowledged fact that the blue-eyed condition was a recessive characteristic. Would it not be the case that the dominant brown-eyed trait would in time supplant the blue-eyed state in the human population? The answer was not self-evident, and Punnett sought out his colleague G. H. Hardy, the astute mathematician at Cambridge University. Hardy had only a passing interest in genetics, but the problem intrigued him as a mathematical one. The solution, which we shall consider below, ranks as one of the most fundamental laws of genetics and evolution. As fate has it, Hardy's formula was arrived at independently in the same year (1908) by a physician, W. Weinberg, and the well-known equation presently bears both their names.

MENDELIAN INHERITANCE

We may recall that the genetic constitutions, or genotypes, of the normal and multilegged frogs have been designated as AA (normal), Aa (normal but a carrier), and aa (multilegged). The kinds and proportions of offspring that can arise from matings involving the three genotypes are illustrated in Figure 4.1. Six different types of matings are possible. The

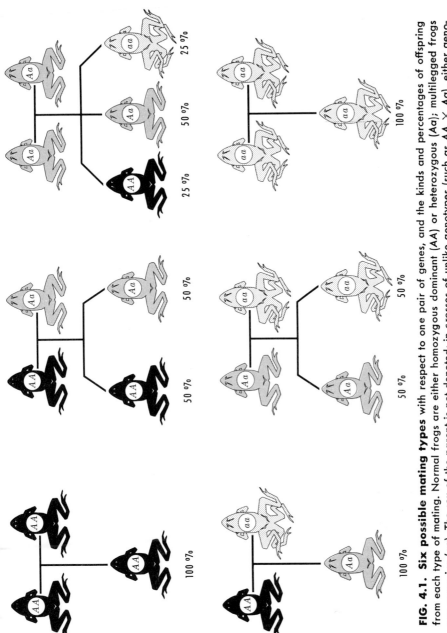

FIG. 4.1. **Six possible mating types** with respect to one pair of genes, and the kinds and percentages of offspring from each type of mating. Normal frogs are either homozygous dominant (AA) or heterozygous (Aa); multilegged frogs are recessive (aa). The sex of the parent is not denoted; in crosses of unlike genotypes (such as AA × Aa), either genotype may be the male or the female.

mating $AA \times AA$ gives rise solely to normal homozygous offspring, AA. Two kinds of progeny, AA and Aa in equal proportions, result from the cross of a homozygous normal parent (AA) and a heterozygous parent (Aa). The mating of two heterozygotes ($Aa \times Aa$) produces AA, Aa, and aa offspring in the classical Mendelian ratio of 1:2:1. Only heterozygous offspring (Aa) emerge from the mating $AA \times aa$. Both heterozygous (Aa) and recessive (aa) progeny, in equal numbers, arise from the cross of a heterozygous parent (Aa) and a recessive parent (aa). Lastly, two recessive parents ($aa \times aa$) produce only recessive offspring (aa).

These principles of Mendelian inheritance merely inform us that certain kinds of offspring can be expected from certain types of matings. If we are interested in following the course of a population from one generation to the next, then additional factors enter the scene.

RANDOM MATING

One important factor that influences the genetic composition of a population is the system of mating among individuals. The simplest scheme of breeding activity in a population is referred to as *random mating*, wherein any one individual has an equal chance of pairing with any other individual. Stated another way, the bearer of any given genotype may choose its mate without showing preference for a particular genotype.

The absence of preferential mating in a population has interesting consequences. Let us suppose that random mating prevails in our particular population of bullfrogs. This assemblage of frogs is ordinarily very large, numbering several thousand individuals. For ease of presentation, however, the size of the population may be reduced to 48 males and 48 females. Moreover, of each sex, we may assume that 36 are normal (12 AA and 24 Aa) and 12 are multilegged (aa). Accordingly, one quarter of the individuals of each sex are homozygous dominant, one half are heterozygous, and one quarter are recessive. Now, if mating occurs at random, will the incidence of multilegged frogs decrease, increase, or remain the same in the next generation?

The problem may be approached by determining how often a given type of mating occurs. Here we will introduce one of the cardinal rules of probability: *the chance that two independent events will occur together is the product of their chances of occurring separately.* The proportion of AA males in our arbitrary bullfrog population is $\frac{1}{4}$. We may also say that the chance of a male bullfrog being AA is $\frac{1}{4}$. Likewise the probability that a female bullfrog is AA is $\frac{1}{4}$. Consequently, the chance that an AA male will "occur together," or mate, with an AA female is $\frac{1}{16}$ ($\frac{1}{4} \times \frac{1}{4}$). The computations for all types of matings can be facilitated by coupling the males and females in a multiplication table, as shown in Table 4.1.

TABLE 4.1

Female	Male (♂)		
(♀)	¼ AA	¾ Aa	¼ aa
¼ AA	$\frac{1}{16}$ AA × AA	$\frac{2}{16}$ AA × Aa	$\frac{1}{16}$ AA × aa
¾ Aa	$\frac{2}{16}$ Aa × AA	$\frac{4}{16}$ Aa × Aa	$\frac{2}{16}$ Aa × aa
¼ aa	$\frac{1}{16}$ aa × AA	$\frac{2}{16}$ aa × Aa	$\frac{1}{16}$ aa × aa

Table 4.1 shows that there are nine combinations of mated pairs, and that some types occur more frequently than others. It may be helpful to express the frequencies in terms of actual numbers. Thus, for a total of 48 matings, 3 (= $\frac{1}{16}$ × 48) would be AA ♀ × AA ♂, 6 (= $\frac{2}{16}$ × 48) would be AA ♀ × Aa ♂, 12 (= $\frac{4}{16}$ × 48) would be Aa ♀ × Aa ♂, and so forth. The numbers of each type of mating are listed in Table 4.2.

Our next step is to ascertain the kinds and proportions of offspring from each mating. We shall assume that each mated pair yields the same number of offspring—12, for simplicity. (This is an inordinately small number, as a single female bullfrog can deposit well over 10,000 eggs.) We shall also take for granted that the genotypes of the 12 progeny from each mating are those that are theoretically possible in Mendelian inheritance (see Fig. 4.1). For example, if the parents are Aa × Aa, their offspring will be 3 AA, 6 Aa, and 3 aa. In another instance, if the parents are AA × Aa, then the offspring will be 6 AA and 6 Aa. The outcome of all crosses is shown in Table 4.2. It is important to note that the actual numbers of offspring recorded in Table 4.2 are related to the frequencies

TABLE 4.2

Type of Mating (female × male)	Number of Each Type of Mating*	Number of Offspring		
		AA	Aa	aa
AA × AA	3	36		
AA × Aa	6	36	36	
AA × aa	3		36	
Aa × AA	6	36	36	
Aa × Aa	12	36	72	36
Aa × aa	6		36	36
aa × AA	3		36	
aa × Aa	6		36	36
aa × aa	3			36
		144	288	144
		(25%)	(50%)	(25%)

* Based on a total of 48 matings.

of the different types of matings. For example, the mating of an *AA* female with an *Aa* male occurs six times; hence, the numbers of offspring are increased sixfold (from 6 each of *AA* and *Aa* to 36 each of the two genotypes).

An examination of Table 4.2 reveals that the kinds and proportions of individuals in the new generation of offspring are exactly the same as in the parental generation. There has been no change in the ratio of normal frogs (75 percent *AA* and *Aa*) to multilegged frogs (25 percent *aa*). In fact, the proportions of phenotypes (and genotypes) will remain the same in all successive generations, provided that the system of random mating is continued.

GENE FREQUENCIES

There is a less tedious method of arriving at the same conclusion. Rather than figure out all the matings that can possibly occur, we need only to consider the genes that are transmitted by the eggs and sperms of the parents. Let us assume that each parent produces only 10 gametes. The 12 homozygous dominant males (*AA*) of our arbitrary initial population can contribute 120 sperm cells to the next generation, each sperm containing one *A*. The 24 heterozygous males (*Aa*) can transmit 240 gametes, 120 of them with *A* and 120 with *a*. The remaining 12 recessive males (*aa*) can furnish 120 gametes, each with *a*. The total pool of genes provided by all males will be 240 *A* and 240 *a*, or 50 percent of each kind. Expressed as a decimal fraction, the frequency of gene *A* is 0.5; of *a*, 0.5.

Since the females in our population have the same genetic constitutions as the males, their gametic contribution to the next generation will also be 0.5 *A* and 0.5 *a*. The eggs and sperms can now be united at random in a genetical checkerboard (Fig. 4.2).

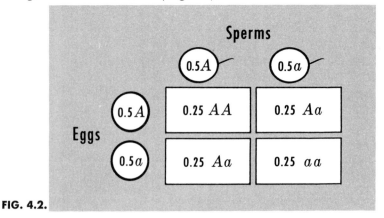

FIG. 4.2.

It should be evident from Figure 4.2 that the distribution of genotypes among the offspring is 0.25 AA : 0.50 Aa : 0.25 aa. The random union of eggs and sperms yields the same result as the random mating of parents (refer to Table 4.2). Thus, using two different approaches, we have answered the question posed in the introductory remarks to this chapter. *If the multi-legged frogs are equally as fertile as the normal frogs and leave equal numbers of offspring each generation, then these anomalous frogs will persist in the population with the same frequency from one generation to the next.*

HARDY-WEINBERG LAW

A population in which the proportions of genotypes remain unchanged from generation to generation is said to be in *equilibrium*. The fact that a system of random mating leads to a condition of equilibrium was brought to light independently by G. H. Hardy and W. Weinberg, and has come to be widely known as the *Hardy-Weinberg Law*. This Law states that the proportions of AA, Aa, and aa genotypes, as well as the proportions of A and a genes, will remain constant from generation to generation provided that the bearers of the three genotypes have equal opportunities of producing offspring in a large, randomly mating population.

The above statement can be translated into a simple mathematical expression. If we let p be the frequency of the gene A in the population, and q equal the frequency of its allele, a, then the distribution of the genotypes in the next generation will be p^2 AA : $2pq$ Aa : q^2 aa. This relationship may be verified by the use, once again, of a genetical checkerboard (Fig. 4.3). Mathematically inclined readers will recognize that p^2 : $2pq$: q^2 is the algebraic expansion of the binomial $(p + q)^2$. The frequencies of the three genotypes (0.25 AA : 0.50 Aa : 0.25 aa) in our bullfrog population under the system of random mating is the expanded binomial $(0.5 + 0.5)^2$.

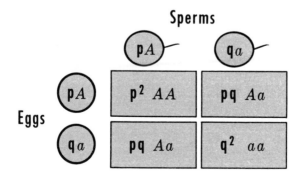

FIG. 4.3.

We may consider another arbitrary population in the equilibrium state. Suppose that the population consists of 16 *AA*, 48 *Aa*, and 36 *aa* individuals. We may assume, as before, that 10 gametes are contributed by each individual to the next generation. All the gametes (numerically, 160) transmitted by the 16 *AA* parents will contain the *A* gene, and half the gametes (240) provided by the *Aa* parents will bear the *A* gene. Thus, of the total of 1,000 gametes, 400 will carry the *A* gene. Accordingly, the frequency of gene *A* is 0.4 (designated p). In like manner, it can be shown that the frequency of gene *a* is 0.6 (q). Substituting the numerical values for p and q in the Hardy-Weinberg formula, we have

$$p^2 \, AA : 2pq \, Aa : q^2 \, aa$$
$$(0.4)^2 \, AA : 2(0.4)(0.6) \, Aa : (0.6)^2 \, aa$$
$$0.16 \, AA : 0.48 \, Aa : 0.36 \, aa$$

Hence, the proportions of the three genotypes are the same as those of the preceding generation.

IMPLICATIONS

The Hardy-Weinberg Law is entirely theoretical. A set of underlying assumptions are made that can scarcely be fulfilled in any natural population. We implicitly assume the absence of recurring mutations, the absence of any degree of preferential matings, the absence of differential mortality or fertility, the absence of immigration or emigration of individuals, and the absence of fluctuations in gene frequencies due to sheer chance. But therein lies the significance of the Hardy-Weinberg Law. In revealing the conditions under which evolutionary change cannot occur, it brings to light the forces that could operate to cause a change in the genetic composition of a population. The Hardy-Weinberg Law thus depicts a static situation. There are several factors or forces that profoundly modify the gene frequencies in natural populations. In the next chapter, we shall consider how one of the forces, natural selection, or differential reproduction, can lead to dynamic evolutionary changes.

It should also be clear that a recessive trait, such as blue eyes in man, is not destined to become rare because it happens to be governed by a recessive gene. Nor can the dominant brown-eyed condition become widespread simply by virtue of its dominance. Whether a given gene is common or rare is controlled by other factors, prominent among them being natural selection.

SUGGESTIONS FOR FURTHER READING

DUNN, L. C. and DOBZHANSKY, T. 1952. *Heredity, race, and society.* New York: New American Library of World Literature, Inc.
STERN, C. 1943. The Hardy-Weinberg law. *Science* 97: 137–138.
———. 1960. *Principles of human genetics.* San Francisco: W. H. Freeman & Co., Publishers.

5 Concept of Selection

We have already remarked that the multilegged anomaly, which appeared in 1958 in a local bullfrog population, has not been detected since that occasion. The supposition was made that the multilegged trait was governed by a recessive mutant gene. Some of us might presume that the mutant gene responsible for the abnormality has disappeared entirely from the population. But can a detrimental mutant gene be completely eradicated from natural populations of organisms, even in the face of the severest form of selection? Most persons are frankly puzzled when they are informed that the answer is *"No."* Yet our knowledge of the properties of mutation and selection expressly permits a firm negative reply.

SELECTION AGAINST RECESSIVE DEFECTS

In our consideration of the Hardy-Weinberg Law in the preceding chapter, we assumed that the mutant multilegged frogs (*aa*) were as reproductively fit as their normal kin (*AA* and *Aa*) and left equal numbers of living offspring each generation. Now, however, let us presume that all multilegged individuals fail to reach sexual maturity generation after generation. Will the incidence of the multilegged trait decline to a vanishing point?

We may start with the same distribution of individuals in the initial generation as had been previously postulated in chapter 4; namely, 24 *AA*, 48 *Aa*, and 24 *aa*, with the sexes equally represented. Since the multilegged frogs (*aa*) are unable to participate in breeding, the parents of the next generation comprise only the 24 *AA* and 48 *Aa* individuals. The heterozygous types are twice as numerous as the homozygous dominants; accordingly, two–thirds of the total breeding members of the population are *Aa* and one–third are *AA*. We may once again employ a genetical checkerboard

(Table 5.1) to ascertain the different types of matings and their relative frequencies.

TABLE 5.1

Female (♀)	Male (♂)	
	⅓ AA	⅔ Aa
⅓ AA	⅑ AA × AA	²⁄₉ AA × Aa
⅔ Aa	²⁄₉ Aa × AA	⁴⁄₉ Aa × Aa

The frequencies of the different matings shown in Table 5.1 may be expressed as whole numbers rather than fractions. Given a total of 36 matings, 4 (= ⅑ × 36) would be AA ♀ × AA ♂, 8 (= ²⁄₉ × 36) would be AA ♀ × Aa ♂, 8 (= ²⁄₉ × 36) would be Aa ♀ × AA ♂, and 16 (= ⁴⁄₉ × 36) would be Aa ♀ × Aa ♂. These numbers are recorded in Table 5.2.

Our next task is to determine the outcome of each type of cross. We shall assume that each mated pair contributes an equal number of progeny to the next generation (say, 12). As revealed in Table 5.2, the offspring are distributed according to Mendelian ratios, and the actual numbers of offspring reflect the frequencies of the different kinds of matings. For example, a single AA ♀ × Aa ♂ mating yields 12 offspring in the Mendelian ratio of 6 AA : 6 Aa. There are, however, eight matings of this kind; the numbers of offspring are correspondingly increased to 48 AA and 48 Aa.

TABLE 5.2

Type of Mating (female × male)	Number of Each Type of Mating*	Number of Offspring		
		AA	Aa	aa
AA × AA	4	48		
AA × Aa	8	48	48	
Aa × AA	8	48	48	
Aa × Aa	16	48	96	48
		192	192	48
		(44.44%)	(44.44%)	(11.11%)

* Based on a total of 36 matings.

Even though all the multilegged frogs fail to reproduce, the abnormal recessive genes are still transmitted to the first generation. The emergence of multilegged frogs in the first generation stems, of course, from the matings of two heterozygous frogs. However, as seen from Table 5.2, the frequency of the multilegged trait (aa) decreases from 25 percent to 11.11 percent in a single generation.

The effects of complete selection against the multilegged frogs in subsequent generations can be determined by the foregoing method of calculation, but the lengthy tabulations tend to become wearisome. At this point we may apply a formula which will enable us to establish in a few steps the frequency of the recessive gene after any number of generations of complete selection. This modest formula is

$$q_n = \frac{q_o}{1 + nq_o}$$

In the above expression, q_o represents the initial or original frequency of the recessive gene, and q_n is the frequency after n generations. Thus, with the initial value of $q_o = 0.5$, the frequency of the recessive gene after two generations ($n = 2$) will be

$$q_2 = \frac{q_o}{1 + 2q_o} = \frac{0.5}{1 + 2(0.5)} = \frac{0.5}{2.0} = 0.25$$

If the frequency of the recessive gene itself (a) is q, then the frequency of the recessive individual (aa) is q^2. Accordingly, the frequency of the recessive homozygote is $(0.25)^2$, or 0.0625 (6.25 percent). In the second generation, therefore, the incidence of the multilegged trait drops to 6.25 percent.

If we perform comparable calculations through several generations, we emerge with a picture that is portrayed in Figure 5.1. In the third gen-

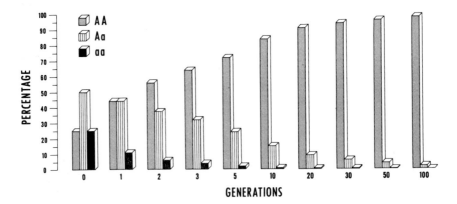

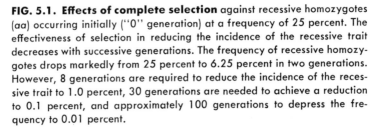

FIG. 5.1. Effects of complete selection against recessive homozygotes (*aa*) occurring initially (''0'' generation) at a frequency of 25 percent. The effectiveness of selection in reducing the incidence of the recessive trait decreases with successive generations. The frequency of recessive homozygotes drops markedly from 25 percent to 6.25 percent in two generations. However, 8 generations are required to reduce the incidence of the recessive trait to 1.0 percent, 30 generations are needed to achieve a reduction to 0.1 percent, and approximately 100 generations to depress the frequency to 0.01 percent.

eration, the frequency of the recessive homozygote declines to 4.0 percent. Progress in terms of the elimination of the multilegged trait is initially rapid, but becomes slower as selection is continued over many successive generations. About 20 generations are required to depress the incidence of the multilegged trait to 2 in 1,000 individuals (0.20 percent). Ten additional generations are necessary to effect a reduction to one in a thousand individuals (0.10 percent). Thus, as a recessive trait becomes rarer, selection against it becomes less effective. The reason is quite simple: only very few recessive homozygotes are exposed to the action of selection. The now rare recessive gene (a) is carried mainly by heterozygous individuals (Aa), where it is sheltered from selection by its normal dominant partner (A).

SIGNIFICANCE OF THE HETEROZYGOTES

When the frequency of an abnormal recessive gene becomes very low, most affected offspring (aa) will come from matings of two heterozygous carriers (Aa). For example, in the human population, the vast majority of newly arising albino individuals (aa) in a given generation (more than 99 percent of them) will come from normally pigmented heterozygous parents. It was considerations of this kind that led us to postulate in chapter I that the multilegged frogs that appeared suddenly in the natural population were derived from normal-legged heterozygous parents (refer to Fig. 1.4).

There is no question that detrimental recessive genes in a population are harbored mostly in the heterozygous state. Moreover, the heterozygous carriers (Aa) generally cannot be distinguished from the normal homozygotes or noncarriers (AA). These facts militate against any scheme aimed at completely eradicating an undesirable genetic trait in a population, whether it be a population of fish, fowl, or man.

TABLE 5.3 *Frequencies of Recessive Homozygotes and Carriers*

Frequency of homozygotes (aa)	Frequency of heterozygous carriers (Aa)	Ratio of carriers to homozygotes
1 in 25 (sickle-cell anemia)	1 in 3	8:1
1 in 1,000 (cystic fibrosis)	1 in 16	60:1
1 in 20,000 (albinism)	1 in 70	285:1
1 in 40,000 (phenylketonuria)	1 in 100	400:1
1 in 1,000,000 (alkaptonuria)	1 in 500	2,000:1

It bears emphasizing that the rarity of a recessive disorder does not signify a comparable rarity of heterozygous carriers. Table 5.3 shows that the ratio of heterozygotes to affected persons rises as the recessive trait becomes rarer. Thus, an extremely rare disorder, like alkaptonuria (blackening of urine), occurs in 1 in one million persons. The detrimental recessive gene, however, is carried heterozygously by 1 out of 500 persons. There are 2,000 as many carriers as there are individuals afflicted with the recessive defect.

INTERPLAY OF MUTATION AND SELECTION

Theoretically, if the process of complete selection against the recessive homozygote were to continue for several hundred more generations, then the abnormal recessive gene would be completely eliminated, and the population would consist uniformly of normal homozygotes (AA). But, *in reality*, the steadily diminishing supply of abnormal recessive genes is continually being replenished by recurrent mutations from normal (A) to abnormal (a). Mutations from A to a, which inevitably occur from time to time, were not taken into account in our determinations above. Mutations, of course, cannot be ignored.

All genes undergo mutation at some definable rate. If a certain proportion of A genes are converted into a alleles in each generation, then the population will at all times carry a certain amount of the recessive mutant gene (a) despite selection against it. Without entering into any sophisticated calculations, it can be shown that a point will be reached when the number of the abnormal recessive genes eliminated by selection just balances the number of the same recessive gene produced by mutation. An analogy shown in Figure 5.2A will help in visualizing this circumstance. The water level in the beaker remains constant when the rate at which water enters the opening of the beaker equals the rate at which it leaves the hole in the side of the beaker. In other words, a state of equilibrium is reached when the rate at which the recessive gene is replenished by mutation equals the rate at which it is lost by selection. It should be clear that it is not mutation alone that governs the incidence of deleterious recessives in a population. The generally low frequency of harmful recessive genes stems from the dual action of mutation and selection. The mutation process tends to increase the number of detrimental recessives; the selection mechanism is the counteracting agent.

What would be the consequences of an increase in the mutation rate? Man today lives in an environment in which high-energy radiation promotes a higher incidence of mutations. We may return to our analogy (Fig. 5.2B). The increased rate of mutation may be envisioned as an increased input of water. The water level in the beaker will rise and water will escape

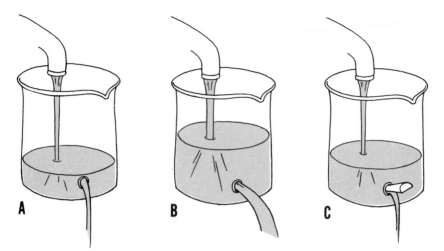

FIG. 5.2. Interplay of detrimental mutant genes (water from faucet) and their elimination by selection (water escaping through hole) in a population (beaker) containing a pool of the harmful genes (water in beaker). *A.* State of genetic equilibrium (constant water level in beaker) when the rates at which water enters and leaves the beaker are equal. *B.* Effect of an increase in mutation rate (increased flow of faucet water) as might be expected from the continued widespread use of ionizing radiation. A new equilibrium (new constant water level) is established, but the frequency of the detrimental gene in the population is higher (higher water level in beaker). *C.* Effect of reducing selection pressure (decreased exit of water) as a consequence of improving the reproductive fitness of genetically defective individuals by modern medical practices. Mutation rate (inflow of water) is the same as in *A.* The inevitable result is a greater incidence of the harmful mutant gene in the population (higher level of water in the beaker).

more rapidly through the hole in the side of the beaker. Similarly, mutant genes will be found more frequently in a population, and they will be eliminated at a faster rate from the population. As before, a balance will be restored eventually between mutation and selection, but now the population has a larger store of deleterious genes and a larger number of defective individuals arising each generation.

The supply of defective genes in the human population has already increased through the greater medical control of recessive disorders. The outstanding advances in modern medicine have served to prolong the lives of genetically defective individuals who might otherwise not have survived to reproductive age. This may be compared to partially plugging the hole in the side of the beaker (Fig. 5.2C). The water level in the beaker will obviously rise, as will the amount of deleterious genes in a population. Evidently, the price of our humanitarian principles is the enlargement of our pool of defective genes.

PARTIAL SELECTION

We have treated above the severest form of selection against recessive individuals. Complete, or 100 percent, selection against a recessive homozygote is often termed lethal selection, and the mutant gene is designated as a lethal gene. A lethal gene does not necessarily result in the death of the individual, but does effectively prevent him from reproducing or leaving offspring. Not all mutant genes are lethal; in fact, the majority of them have less drastic effects on viability or fertility. A mildly handicapped recessive homozygote may reproduce but may be inferior in fertility to the normal individual. When the reproductive capacity of the recessive homozygote is only half as great as the normal type, he is said to be semisterile and the mutant gene is classified as semilethal. A subvital recessive gene is one which, in double dose, impairs an individual to the extent that his reproductive fitness is less than 100 percent but more than 50 percent of normal proficiency.

The action of selection varies correspondingly with the degree of detrimental effect of the recessive gene. Figure 5.3 shows the results of different intensities of selection in a population that initially contains 1.0 percent recessive homozygotes. With complete (lethal) selection, a reduction in the incidence of the recessive trait from 1.0 percent to 0.25 percent is accomplished in 10 generations. Twenty generations of complete selection reduces the incidence to 0.11 percent. When the recessive gene is semilethal (50 percent selection), 20 generations, or twice as many generations as under complete selection, are required to depress the frequency of the recessive homozygote to about 0.25 percent. Selection against a subvital gene (*e.g.*, 10 percent selection) results in a considerably slower rate of elimination of the recessive homozygotes. When the homozygote is at a very slight reproductive disadvantage (1.0 percent selection), only a small decline of 0.03 percent (from 1.0 percent to 0.97 percent) occurs after 20 generations. It is evident that mildly harmful recessive genes may remain in a population for a long time.

SELECTION AGAINST DOMINANT DEFECTS

If complete selection acts against an abnormal trait caused by a dominant gene (*A*), so that none of the *AA* or *Aa* individuals leave any progeny, then all the *A* genes are at once eliminated. In the absence of recurrent

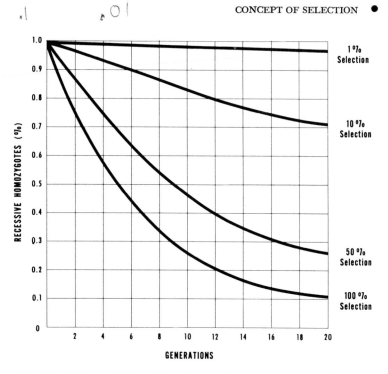

FIG. 5.3. **Different intensities of selection** against recessive homozygotes occurring initially ("0" generation) at a frequency of 1.0 percent. The elimination of recessive individuals per generation proceeds at a slower pace as the strength of selection decreases.

mutation, all subsequent generations will consist exclusively of homozygous recessives (*aa*).

However, we must contend again with ever-occurring mutations and the effects of partial selection. The geneticist Curt Stern of the University of California provides us with a simple, clear model of this situation. Imagine a population of 500,000 individuals, all of whom initially are homozygous recessive (*aa*). Thus, no detrimental dominant genes (*A*) are present as yet and the population as a whole contains 1,000,000 recessive *a* genes. In the first generation, 10 dominant mutant genes arise, as a result of the recessive gene's mutating to the dominant state at a rate of 1 in 100,000 genes. We shall now assume that the dominant mutant gene is semilethal; in other words, only 5 of the newly arisen dominant genes are transmitted to the next, or second, generation. For ease of discussion, this is pictorially represented in Figure 5.4. It can be seen that the second generation would contain a total of 15 dominant genes—5 brought forth from the first generation and 10 new ones added by mutation. In the third generation, the 5 dominant genes carried over from the first generation would be reduced

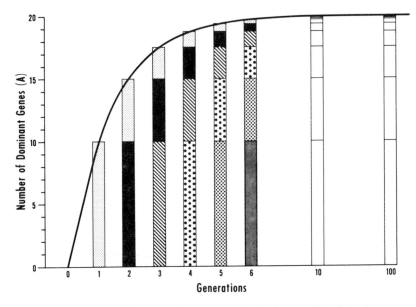

FIG. 5.4. Establishment of a constant level of a semilethal dominant gene (A) in a population over the course of several generations. The fixed number of new dominant genes introduced each generation through mutations from a to A eventually exactly balances the number of dominant genes selectively eliminated each generation. In this particular case, an equilibrium is reached (after about 12 generations) when the total number of dominant genes is approximately 20.

to 2.5, the 10 dominant alleles of the second generation would be depressed to 5, and 10 new abnormal alleles would arise anew by mutation. The total number of dominant genes would increase slightly each subsequent generation, until a point is reached (about 12 generations) where the rate of elimination of the abnormal dominant gene balances the rate of mutation. In other words, the inflow of new dominant alleles by mutation each generation is balanced by the outflow or elimination of the dominant genes each generation by selection.

The equilibrium frequency of the detrimental dominant gene in a population can be altered by changing the rate of loss of the gene in question. In man, retinoblastoma, or cancer of the eye in newborn babies, has until recently been a fatal condition caused by a dominant mutant gene. With modern medical treatment, approximately 70 percent of the afflicted individuals can be saved. The effect of increasing the reproductive fitness of the survivors is to raise the frequency of the abnormal dominant gene in the human population. The accumulation of detrimental genes in the human gene pool is a matter of growing awareness and concern.

CONCEALED VARIABILITY IN NATURAL POPULATIONS

From what we have already learned, we should expect to find in natural populations a large number of deleterious recessive genes concealed in the heterozygous state. It may seem that this expectation is based more on theoretical deduction than on actual demonstration. This is not entirely the case. Penetrating studies by a number of investigators of several species of the fruit fly, Drosophila, have unmistakably disclosed an enormous store of recessive mutant genes harbored by individuals in nature. We may take as an illustrative example the kinds and incidence of recessive genes detected in *Drosophila pseudoobscura* from California populations. The following data are derived from the studies of the noted geneticist Theodosius Dobzhansky, then at Columbia University but later at Rockefeller University in New York.

Flies were collected from nature, and a series of elaborate crosses were performed in the laboratory to yield offspring in which one pair of chromosomes carried an identical set of genes. The formerly hidden recessive genes in a given pair of chromosomes were thus all exposed in the homozygous state. All kinds of recessive genes were uncovered in different chromosomes, as exemplified by those unmasked in one particular chromosome, known simply as the "second." About 33 percent of the second chromosomes harbored one or more recessive genes that proved to be lethal or semilethal to flies carrying the second chromosome in duplicate. An astonishing number of second chromosomes—93 percent of them—contained genes that produced subvital or mildly incapacitating effects when present in the homozygous condition. Other unmasked recessive genes resulted in sterility of the flies or severely retarded the developmental rates of the flies. All these flies were normal in appearance when originally taken from nature. It is apparent that very few, if any, outwardly normal flies in natural populations are free of hidden detrimental recessive genes.

GENETIC LOAD IN HUMAN POPULATIONS

The study of the concealed variability, or genetic load, in man cannot be approached, for obvious reasons, by the experimental breeding techniques used with fruit flies. Estimates of the genetic load in the human population have been based principally on the incidence of defective offspring from marriages of close relatives (consanguineous marriages). It can be safely stated that every human individual contains at least one newly mutated gene. It can also be accepted that any crop of gametes contains, in addition to one or more mutations of recent origin, at least ten mutant genes that arose in the individuals of preceding generations and which have accumulated in the population. The average person is said to harbor four concealed lethal genes, each of which, if homozygous, is capable of causing death between birth and maturity. The most conservative estimates place the incidence of deformities to detrimental mutant genes in the vicinity of 2 per 1,000 births. *It is evident that man is not uniquely exempt from his share of defective genes.*

SUGGESTIONS FOR FURTHER READING

CROW, J. F. 1959. Ionizing radiation and evolution. *Scientific American,* September, pp. 138–160.

DOBZHANSKY, T. 1950. The genetic basis of evolution. *Scientific American,* January, pp. 32–41.

————. 1961. Man and natural selection. *American Scientist* 49:285–299.

HARDIN, G. 1959. *Nature and man's fate.* New York: New American Library of World Literature, Inc.

MULLER, H. J. 1955. Radiation and human mutation. *Scientific American,* November, pp. 58–68.

REED, S. C. 1964. *Parenthood and heredity.* New York: John Wiley & Sons, Inc.

WALLACE, B. 1970. *Genetic load.* Englewood Cliffs, N.J.: Prentice-Hall, Inc.

WALLACE, B. and DOBZHANSKY, T. 1959. *Radiation, genes, and man.* New York: Holt, Rinehart & Winston, Inc.

6 Selection in Action

The process of evolution is slow and continuous. We have seen that many generations of persistent selection are required to reduce drastically the frequency of an unfavorable mutant gene in a population. Likewise, it generally takes an inordinately long period of time for a new favorable mutant gene to replace its allele throughout a large population. Yet, we have encountered situations in nature in which a favorable mutation has spread through a population in a comparatively short span of years. We shall direct our attention to some outstanding examples in which man has actually observed evolution in progress.

INDUSTRIAL MELANISM

One of the most spectacular evolutionary changes witnessed by man has been the emergence and predominance in recent times of dark, or melanic, varieties of moths in the industrial areas of England and continental Europe. Slightly more than a century ago dark-colored moths were exceptional. The typical moth in the early 1800's was characterized by a light color pattern, which blended with the light coloration of tree trunks on which the moths alighted. But then the Industrial Revolution intervened to alter materially the character of the countryside. As soot and other industrial wastes poured over rural areas, the vegetation became increasingly coated and darkened by black smoke particles. In areas heavily contaminated with soot, the formerly abundant light-colored moths have been supplanted by the darker varieties. This dramatic change in the coloration of moths has been termed "industrial melanism." At least 70 species of moths in England have been affected by man's disturbance of the environment.

During the past two decades, several scientists, particularly E. B. Ford and H. B. D. Kettlewell at the University of Oxford, have analyzed the phenomenon of industrial melanism. Kettlewell photographed the light and dark forms of the peppered moth, *Biston betularia,* against two different backgrounds (Fig. 6.1). The light variety is concealed and the dark

FIG. 6.1. Dark and light forms of the peppered moth (*Biston betularia*) clinging to a soot-blackened oak tree in Birmingham, England (left), and to a light, lichen-coated oak tree in an unpolluted region (*right*). (Courtesy of Dr. H. B. D. Kettlewell.)

form is clearly visible when the moths rest on a light lichen-coated trunk of an oak tree in an unpolluted rural district. Against a sooty black oak trunk, the light form is conspicuous and the dark form is well camouflaged. Records of the dark form of the peppered moth date back to 1848, when its occurrence was reported at Manchester in England. At that time, the dark form comprised less than 1 percent of the population. By 1898, only 50 years later, the dark form had come to dominate the Manchester locale, having attained a remarkably high frequency estimated at 95 percent. In fact, the incidence of the melanic type has reached 90 percent or more in most British industrial areas.

The rapid spread of the dark variety of moth is explicitly intelligible. The dark variants are protectively colored in the smoke-polluted industrial regions. They more easily escape detection by predators, namely insect-eating birds. Actual films taken by Kettlewell and Niko Tinbergen reveal that birds prey on the moths in a selective manner. That is to say, predatory birds more often capture the conspicuous light-colored moths in polluted woodlands. In a single day, the numbers of light forms in an industrial area may be pared by as much as one-half by bird predation.

Experimental breeding tests have demonstrated that the two varieties differ principally by a single gene, the dark variant being dominant to the light one. The dominant mutant gene was initially disadvantageous and probably was maintained at an extremely low frequency in nature by a balance between mutation and selection (see chapter 5). Then, as an indirect consequence of industrialization, the mutant gene became favored by natural selection and spread rapidly in populations in a comparatively short period of time. In unpolluted or non-industrial areas in western England and northern Scotland, the dominant mutant gene does not confer an advantage on its bearers and the light recessive moth remains the prevalent type.

One of the many impressive features of Kettlewell's studies lies in the unequivocal identification of the selecting agent. Selection, we may recall, has been defined as differential reproduction. The act of selection in itself does not reveal the factors or agencies that enable one genotype to leave more offspring than another. We may demonstrate the existence of selection, yet remain baffled as to the precise causative agent of selection. We might have reasonably suspected that predatory birds were directly responsible for the differential success of the melanic forms in survival and reproduction, but Kettlewell's laboriously accumulated data provided that all-important, often elusive, ingredient: *proof.*

AUSTRALIAN RABBITS

The European wild rabbit, *Oryctolagus cuniculus*, has gained infamous notoriety in Australia as the most serious economic pest ever introduced on this isolated island continent. In 1859, a small colony of 24 wild rabbits was brought from Europe to an estate in Victoria in the southeastern corner of Australia. From such modest beginnings, the rabbits proliferated rapidly and by 1928 had spread over the greater part of the Australian continent. Estimates placed the number of adult rabbits at over 500 million in an area of about one million square miles. In overrunning the open grassy plains, the rabbits have caused extensive deterioration to sheepgrazing pastures and to wheat fields.

For many years, the Australian government spent large sums of money on various measures to control the population explosion of these prolific animals. Trapping, "rabbit-proof" fencing, poisoning of water holes, and fumigation all proved to be largely ineffectual. Then, beginning in 1950, outstanding success in decimating the rabbit population was achieved by inoculating rabbits with a virus that causes the fatal disease myxomatosis. The deadly virus was implanted into the tissues of rabbits in the southern area of Australia. In a remarkably short period of time, the virus had made its way, aided by insect carriers (mosquitoes), into most of the rabbit populations throughout the continent. By 1953, from 80 to 90 percent of the rabbit population in Australia had been annihilated.

However, after their drastic decline in the early 1950's the rabbit populations began to build up again. Mutations conferring resistance to the myxomatosis virus have selectively accumulated in the rabbit populations. Today the multiplication of these genetically resistant strains of rabbits is uncontrollable. Moreover, there is also evidence that the viruses themselves have undergone genetic changes. Strains of viruses have evolved that are less virulent to the rabbits. The less virulent viruses enjoy a selective advantage, since their own chances of surviving are enhanced if they do not cause instantaneous death of the host rabbits. The longer the virus remains in the host, the greater the opportunity for that virus to be transferred by mosquitoes to other, uninfected rabbits.

SELECTION FOR RESISTANCE

Penicillin, sulfonamides (sulfa drugs), streptomycin, and other modern antibiotic agents made front-page headlines when first introduced. These wonder drugs were exceptionally effective against certain disease-producing bacteria, and contributed immeasurably to the saving of human lives in World War II. However, the effectiveness of these drugs has been reduced by the emergence of resistant strains of bacteria. Medical authorities regard the rise of resistant bacteria as the most serious development in the field of infectious diseases over the past decade. Bacteria now pass on their resistance to antibiotics faster than people spread the infectious bacteria.

Mutations have occurred in bacterial populations that enable the mutant bacterial cells to survive in the presence of the drug. Here again we notice that mutations furnish the source of evolutionary changes, and that the fate of the mutant gene is governed by selection. In a normal environment, mutations that confer resistance to a drug are rare or undetected. In an environment changed by the addition of a drug, the drug-resistant mutants are favored and supplant the previously normal bacterial strains.

It might be thought that the mutations conferring resistance are actually caused or induced by the drug. This is not the case. Drug-resistant mutations arise in bacterial cells irrespective of the presence or absence of the drug. An experiment developed by the Stanford University geneticist Joshua Lederberg provides evidence that the drug acts as a selecting

SPONTANEOUS ORIGIN OF MUTATION

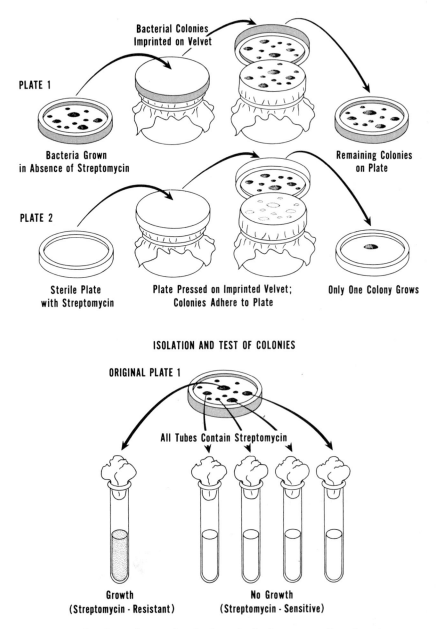

FIG. 6.2. Experiment by Joshua Lederberg revealing that drug-resistant mutations in bacterial cells had not been induced by the drug but had already been present prior to exposure of the bacteria to the drug.

agent permitting preexisting mutations to express themselves. As seen in Figure 6.2, colonies of bacteria were grown on a streptomycin-free agar medium in a petri plate. When the agar surface of this plate was pressed gently on a piece of sterile velvet, some cells from each bacterial colony clung to the fine fibers of the velvet. The imprinted velvet could now be used to transfer the bacterial colonies onto a second agar plate. In fact, more than one replica of the original bacterial growth can be made by pressing several agar plates on the same area of velvet. This ingenious technique has been appropriately called *replica plating*.

In preparing the replicas, Lederberg used agar plates containing streptomycin. Of course, on these agar plates, only bacterial colonies re-sistant to streptomycin grew. In the case depicted in Figure 6.2, one colony was resistant. Significantly, this one resistant colony was found in the same exact position in all replica plates. If mutations arose in response to exposure to a drug, it is hardly to be expected that mutant bacterial colonies would arise in precisely the same site on each occasion. In other words, a haphazard or random distribution of resistant bacterial colonies, without restraint or attention to location in the agar plate, would be expected if the mutations did not already exist in the original bacterial colonies.

Now, we can return to the original plate, as did Lederberg, and test samples of the original bacterial colonies in a test tube for sensitivity or resistance to streptomycin (bottom part of Fig. 6.2). It is noteworthy that the bacterial colonies on the original plate had not been previously in con-tact with the drug. When these original colonies were isolated and tested for resistance to streptomycin, only one colony proved to be resistant. This one colony occupied a position on the original plate identical with the site of the resistant colony on the replica plates. The experiment demonstrated conclusively that the mutation had not been induced by streptomycin but had already been present before exposure to the drug.

Other genetic changes perpetuated by selection have been detected in recent years. The insecticide with the awesome name of dichloro-diphenyl-trichloroethane, or DDT, was initially highly poisonous to malaria-carrying mosquitoes and typhus-carrying lice. However, in the 27 years since the introduction of this insect poison, numerous mutant DDT-resistant strains of mosquitoes and lice have appeared in widely different parts of the world. Similarly, hydrogen cyanide has for many years been an efficient fumigant in the destruction of insect pests, particularly the scale insect, in the citrus-producing areas of southern California. Mutant strains of scale insects that can tolerate the usual lethal doses of hydrogen cyanide have recently arisen in several of the fruit orchards of California. Man's struggle against diseases and insect pests is unending as long as the mutation process continually produces variants that may have survival value in an altered environment.

Parenthetically, it should be noted that DDT has fallen into increasing disfavor as a threat to wildlife. DDT is an insoluble compound, and retains its chemical potency for many years, rather than breaking down harmlessly within a few days after application. The tenacious DDT can be found today in varied concentrations almost everywhere in the world environment. Residues of DDT have been found in the tissues of the bald eagles in the Arctic, penguins in the Antarctic, and fishes in the Pacific coastal area and lakes of North America. The numbers of brown pelicans in an island colony off the California coast have been critically reduced by the effects of DDT. Eggs deposited by these rare birds have been abnormally fragile with intolerable amounts of DDT in the yolks. In 1969, only a few embryos hatched successfully; most eggs collapsed with weakened shells. Even with the curbed use of DDT in several countries (Sweden, Canada, and the United States), it would take at least a decade for the environment to purge itself of this extremely long-lasting pollutant.

ARTIFICIAL SELECTION

The extensive domestication of animals and plants brought about by man's conscious efforts prompted Charles Darwin to remark that "the power of this principle of selection is not hypothetical." Throughout the ages, man has served as a powerful selecting agent in modifying wild species of animals and plants to suit his needs and whims. When man practices artificial selection, it is he, rather than nature, that determines which characteristics are to be incorporated or discarded in his domesticated stocks. Aritificial selection has been the means of perfecting the sleek Arabian race horse, the toylike Shetland pony, the great Dane, and a vast horde of cultivated crops and ornamental plants.

Skilled herdsmen have combined hybridization and selection to improve their domestic strains of animals. In modern times, a new breed of beef cattle, the Santa Gertrudis, has been developed in the United States at the famous King Ranch of Texas. Cattle of the Santa Gertrudis breed are admirably adapted to the hot, humid conditions prevailing in the Gulf Coast area of the United States. The sturdy Santa Gertrudis breed is a product of 30 years or more of a planned program of careful selective breeding of cattle resulting initially from a cross between Shorthorn and Brahman stocks (Fig. 6.3). The American Brahman, characterized by a prominent hump on its shoulders, is a descendant of the heat-tolerant Zebu, native to India. The Santa Gertrudis combines the Zebu's resistance to heat and the Shorthorn's high beef productivity. The Shorthorn itself is an ex-

Shorthorn

Santa Gertrudis

Brahman

FIG. 6.3. Evolution under Domestication. Selection in the hands of man has led to a new breed of cattle, the Santa Gertrudis, a line initiated by hybridization between the Shorthorn and the Brahman.

cellent example of improvement of beef productivity by selection within a breed. In fact, the Shorthorn is a dual-purpose breed. Strains of Shorthorns have been selected for milk production, as well as beef.

Horticulturists have obtained improved varieties of fruits by crossing plants from different parts of the world. The common cultivated variety of the strawberry owes its origin to a cross between two wild American species, *Fragaria virginiana,* the meadow strawberry of eastern North America, and *Fragaria chiloensis,* the beach strawberry native from Alaska to California and the coast of southern Chile. Ironically, the crosses between these two species were first made in Europe. In 1714, the naturalist M. Frezier, impressed with the exceptionally large fruit of the beach strawberry growing in Chile, returned to Europe with several plants of this strawberry. Plants of the eastern North American strawberry had been already cultivated in European gardens, and hybridizations between the two species gave rise to our modern garden strawberry.

Man has been eminently adept at manipulating and remolding the genetic architecture of his domestic animals and plants. These cultivated types for the most part live in an artificial environment contrived by man. The highly domesticated strains of animals and plants are only as successful as man permits. Incidentally, the same might be said of man himself, for he too is a domestic animal, living in an environment largely of his own making.

SUGGESTIONS FOR FURTHER READING

DOBZHANSKY, T. 1950. The genetic basis of evolution. *Scientific American,* January, pp. 32–41.

DOWDESWELL, W. H. 1960. *The mechanism of evolution.* New York: Harper & Row, Publishers.

HUXLEY, J. 1953. *Evolution in action.* New York: New American Library of World Literature, Inc.

FORD, E. B. 1960. *Mendelism and evolution.* London: Methuen & Co., Ltd.

KETTLEWELL, H. B. D. 1959. Darwin's missing evidence. *Scientific American,* March, pp. 48–53.

RYAN, F. J. 1953. Evolution observed. *Scientific American,* October, pp. 78–83.

TAX, S. (ed.). 1960. *Evolution after Darwin* (3 vols.). Chicago: University of Chicago Press.

Balanced Polymorphism

The concepts presented in the preceding chapters have led us to believe that selection operates at all times to reduce the frequency of an abnormal gene to a low equilibrium level. This view is not entirely accurate. We are aware of genes with deleterious effects that occur at fairly high frequencies in natural populations. A striking instance is the high incidence in certain human populations of a mutant gene that causes a curious and usually fatal form of blood cell destruction, known as sickle-cell anemia. It might be presumed that this detrimental gene is maintained at a high frequency by an exceptionally high mutation rate. There is, however, no evidence to indicate that the sickle-cell gene is unusually mutable. We now know that the maintenance of deleterious genes at unexpectedly high frequencies involves a unique, but not uncommon, selective mechanism, which results in a type of population structure known as *balanced polymorphism*.

SICKLE-CELL ANEMIA

In the early 1900's, an American physician, Dr. James Herrick, observed that the red blood cells of an anemic Negro patient were peculiarly distorted. The red corpuscles were elongated and assumed bizarre sickle-like shapes (Fig. 7.1). This odd anomaly, which occurs predominantly in Negroes, was shown in the 1950's by the human geneticist J. V. Neel of the University of Michigan to be inherited as a simple Mendelian recessive character. The abnormal recessive gene, which, for simplicity, may be designated *a*, alters the configuration of the hemoglobin molecule, the oxygen-carrying component of the red corpuscle. Individuals homozygous for the variant gene (*aa*) are severely afflicted with sickle-cell anemia and usually die in childhood. The red corpuscles of heterozygous persons

(*Aa*) have normal disk shapes, but these cells can be induced, by lowering the oxygen tension, to develop a mildly sickled appearance. The benign heterozygous state is referred to as the sickle-cell trait. The sickling phenomenon is not present in individuals homozygous for *AA*.

In 1949, the distinguished chemist Linus Pauling presented evidence that the hemoglobin molecule in sickle-cell anemic patients is biochemically abnormal. Pauling and his associates used the then relatively new technique of electrophoresis, which characterizes proteins according to

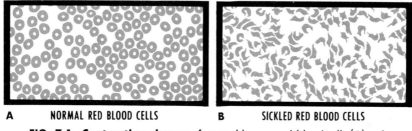

A   NORMAL RED BLOOD CELLS   B   SICKLED RED BLOOD CELLS

FIG. 7.1. **Contrasting shapes** of normal human red blood cells (A) and the peculiar red blood cells of a person afflicted with sickle-cell anemia (B).

the manner in which they move in an electric field. The hemoglobin molecule travels toward the positive pole. The speed of migration of the sickle-cell's hemoglobin differs from that of normal hemoglobin; it moves slower than the normal molecule (Fig. 7.2). The abnormal gene (*a*) thus functions differently from the normal gene (*A*), and, in fact, appears to act independently of its normal partner allele. The heterozygote (*Aa*) does not produce an intermediate product, but rather elaborates both kinds of hemoglobin—the normal type and the sickle-cell anemia variety—in

HEMOGLOBIN ELECTROPHORETIC PATTERN

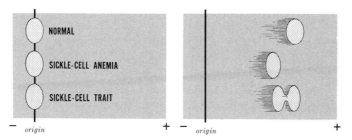

FIG. 7.2. **Electrophoretic patterns of hemoglobins.** The hemoglobin of the heterozygous person with sickle-cell trait is not intermediate in character, but, rather, is composed of approximately equal proportions of the normal hemoglobin and the sickle-cell anemia variety. (Based on studies by Linus Pauling.)

nearly equal quantities (Fig. 7.2). The dual electrophoretic pattern of hemoglobin from a heterozygous individual (*Aa*) can actually be duplicated experimentally by mechanically mixing the hemoglobins taken from blood cells of a normal person (*AA*) and a sickle-cell anemic patient (*aa*). The mixed solution separates in an electric field into the same two hemoglobin components as those characteristic of a person with the sickle-cell trait.

The sickle-cell mutant gene modifies the molecular structure of hemoglobin, and sickle-cell anemia has been appropriately described as a *molecular disease*. It remained for Vernon Ingram at Cambridge University to ascertain how the hemoglobin molecule is altered by the aberrant gene. In 1956, Ingram succeeded in breaking down hemoglobin, a large protein molecule, into several peptide fragments containing short sequences of identifiable amino acids. Normal hemoglobin and sickle-cell hemoglobin yielded the same array of peptide fragments, with a single exception. In one of the peptide fragments of sickle-cell hemoglobin, the amino acid glutamine had been replaced at one point in the chain by valine (Fig. 7.3).

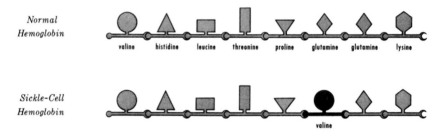

FIG. 7.3. Amino acid sequences in a small section of the normal hemoglobin molecule and of the sickle-cell hemoglobin. The substitution of a single amino acid, glutamine by valine, is responsible for the abnormal sickling of human red blood cells. (Based on studies by Vernon Ingram.)

The sole difference in chemical composition between normal and sickle-cell hemoglobin is the substitution of a single amino acid among several hundred. The fatal effect of sickle-cell anemia is thus traceable to an exceedingly slight alteration in the structure of a protein molecule. The mutation itself probably represents a highly localized change in one of the nucleotide pairs in the chromosomal DNA molecule (refer again to Fig. 3.2).

Since persons with sickle-cell anemia ordinarily do not survive to reproductive age, it might be expected that the abnormal gene would pass rapidly from existence. Each failure of the homozygous anemic individual (*aa*) to transmit his genes would result each time in the loss of two aberrant genes from the population. And yet, the sickle-cell gene reaches remarkably high frequencies in the tropical zone of Africa. In many African populations, 20 percent or more of the individuals have the sickle-cell trait, and frequencies as high as 40 percent have been reported for some African tribes. The sickle-cell trait is not confined to the African continent; it has been found in Sicily and Greece, and in parts of the Near East. What can account for the high incidence of the sickle-cell gene, particularly in light of its detrimental action?

THEORY OF BALANCED POLYMORPHISM

The explanation for the high level of the deleterious sickle-cell gene is to be found in the possibility that the heterozygote (Aa) is superior in fitness to both homozygotes (AA and aa). In other words, selection favors the heterozygote and both types of homozygotes are relatively disadvantageous. Let us examine this form of selection from a theoretical point of view.

Figure 7.4 illustrates the theory. The classical case of selection discussed in preceding chapters is portrayed in the first part of the figure. In this case, when AA and Aa individuals are equal in reproductive fitness, and the aa genotype is completely selected against, the recessive gene will

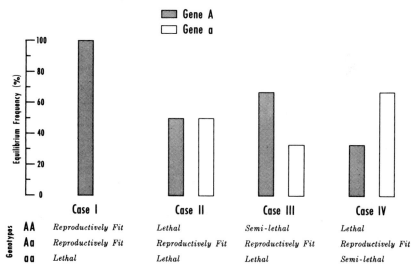

FIG. 7.4. Equilibrium frequencies of two alleles (A and a) under different conditions of selection (ignoring mutation). In contrast to Case I (complete selection and total elimination of a), the recessive gene can be retained at appreciable frequencies in a population when the heterozygote (Aa) is superior in reproductive fitness to *both* homozygotes (Cases II, III, and IV, showing different relative fitnesses of the two homozygotes, AA and aa).

be eliminated. Barring recurring mutations, only A genes will ultimately be present in the population.

Now let us assume (Case II in Fig. 7.4) that both homozygotes (AA as well as aa) are incapable of leaving surviving progeny. The only effective members in the population are the heterozygotes (Aa). Obviously, the frequency of each gene, A and a, will remain at a constant level of 50 percent. The inviability of both homozygous types probably never exists in nature, but the scheme does reveal how two alleles can be maintained at relatively high frequencies. If, as in Case III, the AA genotype leaves only half as many progeny as the heterozygote, and the recessive homozygote is once again inviable, then it is apparent that more A alleles are transmitted each generation than a alleles. Eventually, however, the A gene will reach an equilibrium point at 0.67. Here, it may be noted that, although the recessive homozygote is lethal, the frequency of the recessive allele (a) is maintained at 0.33. In the last illustrative example (Case IV), the recessive homozygote is not as disadvantageous as the dominant homozygote, but both are less reproductively fit than the heterozygote. Here also, both genes remain at relatively high frequencies in the population. Indeed, the recessive allele (a) will comprise 67 percent of the gene pool.

We have thus illustrated in simplified form the nature of the selective forces that serve to maintain two alleles at appreciable frequencies in a population. This phenomenon is known as *balanced polymorphism*. The loss of a deleterious recessive gene through deaths of the homozygotes is balanced by the gain resulting from the larger numbers of offspring produced by the favored heterozygotes.

EXPERIMENTAL VERIFICATION OF BALANCED POLYMORPHISM

A simple experiment, using the fruit fly, *Drosophila melanogaster*, can be performed to demonstrate that an obviously lethal gene can be maintained at a stable, relatively high frequency in a population. The geneticist P. M. Sheppard of the University of Liverpool in England introduced into a breeding cage a population of flies of which 66 percent were normal and 14 percent carried the mutant gene, stubble, which affects the bristles of the fly. The stubble gene is lethal when homozygous; hence, all stubble individuals are heterozygous. Ordinarily the heterozygous fly does not have any reproductive advantage over the normal homozygote. Sheppard, however, created a situation whereby the heterozygote would be favored by removing 60 percent of the normal flies from the population each generation. Consequently, the heterozygote was rendered superior in fitness to either homozygote by virtue of the natural lethality of the stubble homozygote and the enforced reproductive incapacity of many of the normal homozygotes. The results of the experiment are tabulated in Table 7.1.

TABLE 7.1*

Generation	Percentage of stubble flies	Frequency of stubble gene
1	14.3	0.0715
2	33.7	0.1685
3	57.6	0.2880
4	63.2	0.3160
5	69.1	0.3455
6	73.5	0.3675
7	72.9	0.3645
8	73.4	0.3670
9	72.9	0.3645

* From P. M. Sheppard, *Natural Selection and Heredity*, 1959.

It should be noted that the frequency of the stubble gene increased in the early generations, but then became stabilized at a level of about 0.365. The equilibrium level is reached when as many stubble genes are lost from the population, through death of the stubble homozygotes, as are gained as a result of the reproductive advantage of the heterozygote. Although the stubble gene is lethal, the population, under the constant conditions of the experiment, remained at a stable state with a high number of heterozygotes.

The frequency of the stubble gene will fall rapidly when the usual reproductive potential of the normal homozygote is restored. When the normal homozygotes and heterozygotes are equal in reproductive fitness (refer to Case I, Fig. 7.4), the normal gene will supplant the abnormal stubble gene in the population. With these considerations in mind, we shall return to our discussion of sickle-cell anemia.

SUPERIORITY OF THE HETEROZYGOTES

The high frequency of the sickle-cell gene in certain African populations can be explained by assuming that the heterozygotes, *i.e.*, individuals with the sickle-cell trait, have a selective advantage over the normal homozygotes. What might be the nature of the advantage? Field work undertaken in Africa in 1949 by the British geneticist Anthony Allison revealed that the incidence of the sickle-cell trait is high in regions where malignant tertian malaria is endemic. This suggested that there might be an interesting relationship between malaria and the sickle-cell trait. Allison examined blood from African children and found that carriers of the sickle-cell trait were relatively resistant to infection with the parasite *Plasmodium falciparum,* the causative agent of tertian malaria. It would appear, then, that the sickle-cell gene affords some degree of protection for young children against malarial infection. Hence, in areas where malaria is common, children possessing the sickle-cell trait will tend to survive more often than those without the trait, and are more likely to pass on their genes to the next generation. The heterozygotes (*Aa*) are thus superior in fitness to either of the homozygotes (*AA* or *aa*) and a state of balanced polymorphism is established.

Communities in Africa with the greatest reliance on agriculture (rather than on hunting or animal husbandry) tend to have the highest frequencies of the sickle-cell trait. A high incidence of the sickle-cell trait in an intensely malarious environment has the consequence of reducing the number of individuals capable of being infected by the malarial parasite and, accordingly, of lowering the mortality from such infections. More human energy, or greater manpower, is thus made available for raising and harvesting crops. Ironically, then, the sickle-cell trait carries with it the beneficent effect of enabling tribes to develop and maintain an agricultural culture rather than adhere to a hunting or pastoral existence. This is a curious, but striking, instance of the interplay of biological change and socioeconomic adaptation.

We should expect the frequency of the sickle-cell gene to be low in malaria-free areas, where the selective advantage of the heterozygote would be removed. It has been found that the lowest frequencies of the sickle-cell gene occur consistently in regions relatively free of malaria. The frequency of the sickle-cell gene has fallen to low levels in the Negro population of the United States. The frequency of the sickle-cell trait among American Negroes is only about 8 percent. The incidence at birth of the disabling sickle-cell anemia is estimated at two per thousand individuals. Here, as in the case of industrial melanism, man has witnessed a rapid evolutionary change in a population under altered environmental conditions.

INFANTILE AMAUROTIC IDIOCY

An enigmatic subject is the high incidence in human populations of infantile amaurotic idiocy, a fatal recessive disorder. This inherited condition is also known as Tay-Sachs disease, after its co-discoverers, the British ophthalmologist Warren Tay and the American neurologist Bernard Sachs. Affected infants appear normal and healthy at birth, but within six months the nerves of the brain and spinal cord exhibit marked signs of deterioration. The child becomes mentally retarded, progressively blind, and finally paralyzed. The disease take its lethal toll by the age of 3 to 4 years. There are no known survivors and no known cure.

Infantile amaurotic idiocy has been reported from every continent and in most ethnic groups. A feature of special interest, however, is that 9 out of 10 affected children are of Jewish heritage. It is especially common in Jews of northeastern European origin, particularly from provinces in Lithuania and Poland. In the United States, Tay-Sachs disease is about 100 times more prevalent in the Jewish population than among non-Jews. The frequency of heterozygous carriers has been estimated at one in 45 for Jews and one in 350 for non-Jewish Americans. If the high incidence of heterozygotes is maintained by mutation alone, then an extraordinarily high mutation rate of the detrimental recessive gene would have to be postulated. Some reproductive advantage for the heterozygote carrier would seem to be the most plausible explanation, but the nature of this advantage is presently unknown.

SELECTION AGAINST THE HETEROZYGOTE

The discovery of the Rh factor in the 1940's permitted investigators to deduce the real nature of a mother-child blood incompatibility in humans, known as *erythroblastosis fetalis*. Afflicted newborn infants are burdened with anemia, jaundice, enlargement of the liver and spleen, and heart failure. The mother of an erythroblastotic baby is "Rh-negative"— she lacks the Rh factor in her blood cells. The father and the affected child possess the Rh factor and both are accordingly "Rh-positive."

Unknown to the Rh-negative mother, she is immunized (or sensitized) by her own fetus. When the Rh factor of the fetus enters the mother's bloodstream, the Rh-negative mother reacts to the factor as if it were a foreign substance, or antigen. Her body's immune system produces a chemically active substance, or antibody, to attack the antigen, much in the same manner that antibodies fight off infectious bacteria. The mother typically does not build up antibodies in sufficient strength to harm her first infant (Fig. 7.5). But the antibodies remain in her body, and may linger for many months or years. If the second baby is also Rh-positive, the mother's antibodies enter the fetal circulation through the placenta and destroy the fetus' blood cells. The severity of the damage to the fetus ranges from stillbirth to mild anemia at birth, depending on the capacity of the blood-forming tissues of the fetus to compensate by increased production of new blood cells. In most cases, the fetus is unable to offset the large number of red cells destroyed and extreme anemia and other complications result.

The Rh-positive individual has a dominant gene, designated R, which leads to the production of the Rh antigen. The Rh-positive person may be homozygous (RR) or heterozygous (Rr). All Rh-negative individuals carry two recessive genes (rr) and are incapable of producing the Rh antigen.

The inheritance of the Rh factor follows simple Mendelian laws. A mother who is Rh-negative (*rr*) need not fear having erythroblastotic offspring if her husband is likewise Rh-negative (*rr*). If the husband is heterozygous (*Rr*), half of the offspring will be Rh-negative (*rr*) and none of these will be afflicted. The other half will be Rh-positive (*Rr*), just like the father, and are potential victims of the disease. If the Rh-positive father is homozygous dominant (*RR*), then all the children will be Rh-positive (*Rr*) and potential victims. In essence, an Rh-positive child carried by an Rh-negative mother is the setting for possible, though not inevitable, trouble.

Among Caucasians in the United States, the incidence of Rh-negative persons is approximately 16 percent. In certain European groups, such as the Basques in Spain, the frequency of Rh-negative individuals rises as high as 34 percent. Non-Caucasian populations are remarkably relatively free of Rh disease. The incidence of Rh-negative persons among the full-blooded American Indians, Eskimos, African Negro, Japanese, and Chinese is one percent or less. In contrast, the frequency of Rh negativity is high in the American Negro (9 percent), which reflects the historical consequences of intermarriages. The ancestry of the American Negro is approximately one-third Caucasian.

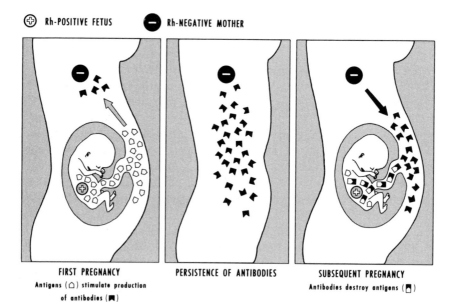

⊕ Rh-POSITIVE FETUS   ⚫ Rh-NEGATIVE MOTHER

FIRST PREGNANCY
Antigens (○) stimulate production of antibodies (🏹)

PERSISTENCE OF ANTIBODIES

SUBSEQUENT PREGNANCY
Antibodies destroy antigens (🏹)

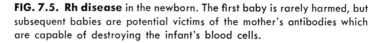

FIG. 7.5. Rh disease in the newborn. The first baby is rarely harmed, but subsequent babies are potential victims of the mother's antibodies which are capable of destroying the infant's blood cells.

It is instructive to calculate the frequencies of risky marriages in Caucasian populations. Table 7.2 shows the different types of marriages that can occur when individuals choose their mates by sheer chance—that is, without regard to each other's Rh makeup. Of the two kinds of marriages that can result in Rh-positive pregnancies, 5.76 percent would be

TABLE 7.2 *Frequencies of Marriages by Chance of Rh-positive and and Rh-negative Individuals in Caucasian Populations*[*]

Female (♀)	Male (♂)		
	36% RR	48% Rr	16% rr
36% RR	12.96% RR × RR	17.28% RR × Rr	5.76% RR × rr
48% Rr	17.28% Rr × RR	23.04% Rr × Rr	7.68% Rr × rr
16% rr	5.76% rr × RR	7.68% rr × Rr	2.56% rr × rr

* Rh-negative persons comprise 16% of the population; among Rh-positive persons, 36% are homozygous dominant and 48% are heterozygous.

rr (females) × *RR* (males) and 7.68 percent would be *rr* (females) × *Rr* (males). Thus approximately 13 percent of all marriages, or one out of every eight, are at a risk with respect to erythroblastosis fetalis.

From the above data, we can ascertain the frequency of potentially dangerous pregnancies. All pregnancies from the *rr* (females) × *RR* (males) would yield an Rh-positive fetus, but only one-half of the infants from the *rr* (females) × *Rr* (males) would be Rh-positive. Thus, the frequency of all potentially troublesome pregnancies is 5.76 + 3.84 = 9.60 percent, or slightly less than one-tenth of all pregnancies.

Theoretically, then, one out of nine or ten pregnancies should result in an erythroblastotic child. However, in actuality, only one in 200 pregnancies results in an afflicted baby. The reasons for the low observed incidence are not entirely clear. Apparently, differences in the ease of sensitization exist among Rh-negative women. The Rh antigen of the fetus may fail to get through the placenta, or some Rh-negative mothers are incapable of responding to the antigen. The low occurrence may also reflect a peculiar protective role of the ABO blood groups in reducing the risk of Rh incompatibility. In 1943, Dr. Philip Levine called attention to the fact that infants of Rh-negative, type O mothers develop Rh disease less often than those of type A or B, Rh-negative mothers. If the infant's red cells are type A or type B, the maternal anti-A and anti-B antibodies in type O women destroy the infant's Rh-positive red cells when they enter the Rh-negative mother's bloodstream. Thus, the invading fetal cells are eliminated before they have the opportunity to sensitize the mother. Ironically, the infant may then suffer from anemia due to the destructive action of the mother's anti-A and anti-B antibodies. The effects of ABO and Rh incompatibilities in combination illustrate the complexities of selective forces: *a double incompatibility clearly affords a lower risk of fetal loss than Rh incompatibility alone.*

Each death of an erythroblastotic infant, who is always heterozygous (*Rr*), results in the elimination of one *R* and one *r* gene. In such a situation where selection continually operates against the heterozygote, the rarer of the two genes should ultimately become lost (or decline to a low level to be maintained solely by mutation). In populations where the *R* gene is much more common than the *r* allele, we should be witnessing a gradual dwindling of the *r* gene.

No decline, however, in the frequency of the *r* gene is in evidence. One counterbalancing factor is the tendency of parents who have lost infants from erythroblastosis to compensate for their losses by having relatively large numbers of children. Thus, if a father is heterozygous (*Rr*) and the mother is homozygous (*rr*), there is an even chance that the infant will be *rr* and unaffected. Each unaffected child born restores two *r* genes lost by the death of two *Rr* erythroblastotic sibs. This consideration alone overrides the selective force against the heterozygote.

In recent years, the management and prevention of Rh disease have advanced considerably. Several hundreds of erythroblastotic infants have been saved by the therapy of "exchange transfusion." This treatment is essentially a flushing-out process, whereby the infant's blood is gradually diluted with donated Rh-negative blood until at the end of the procedure most of the infant's circulating blood is problem-free. In the late 1960's, a vaccine was successfully developed consisting of a blood fraction (gamma globulin) rich in Rh antibodies. Injected into the Rh-negative mother's bloodstream no later than three days after the birth of her first Rh-positive child, the globulin-Rh antibody preparation suppresses the mother's antibody-making activity. We may foresee the end of Rh disease as a major clinical problem. We may also anticipate that the recessive *r* allele will not disappear from the human gene pool, but rather endure.

SELECTIVE ATTRIBUTES OF THE ABO SYSTEM

The recognition that hemolytic disease of the newborn is caused by maternal-fetal incompatibility in the Rh blood group system stimulated a search for evidences of selection in other blood group systems. A wealth of data now reveals that hemolytic disease can be caused by unfavorable antigenic mother-child interactions involving the ABO blood groups. The danger to the unborn child arises when the mother's serum contains an antibody that can be directed against an antigen of the blood cells of her own fetus. If, for example, the infant's red cells are type A (bearing antigen A) and the mother is type O (containing anti-A and anti-B), the maternal anti-A antibody will destroy the infant's A-bearing red cells. Table 7.3 shows that type AB women do not have "incompatible" babies and that type O babies are always "compatible." Clinically, it has been observed that the mother is usually type O, and very seldom type A or B, if her baby has erythroblastosis due to anti-A or anti-B. Anti-A and anti-B in the serum of type O mothers are apparently more potent than the corresponding antibodies in Type A or B mothers.

Erythroblastosis in newborn infants due to anti-A or anti-B is much milder than that caused by anti-Rh, and occurs much less frequently (about 1 in 1,000 pregnancies). However, a disquieting finding in recent years is that anti-A and anti-B manifest their deleterious effects primarily in early pregnancy. There is a significantly greater rate of spontaneous abortions among type O women married to men of type A or B than among A or B women married to O men. In terms of pregnancies terminating prematurely, ABO incompatibility looms more frightening than Rh incompatibility.

TABLE 7.3   *ABO Groups of Mothers and Their Babies*

Mother's Type	Antibodies in Mother's Serum	Types of Incompatible Babies	Types of Compatible Babies
A	anti-B	B, AB	O, A
B	anti-A	A, AB	O, B
AB	none	none	A, B, AB
O	anti-A & anti-B	A, B	O

There is growing evidence that individuals belonging to different ABO groups differ in their susceptibility to certain common diseases. Type O persons are at least 40 percent more prone to develop duodenal ulcers than individuals belonging to groups A, B, or AB. Type O people also have a higher incidence of gastric ulcers. On the other hand, type O individuals are less likely to develop pernicious anemia or cancer of the stomach than type A persons.

The association between diseases and the ABO blood groups is difficult to comprehend or evaluate. Some diseases, such as cancer of the stomach, mainly affect a person beyond the reproductive age, after the person has passed on his genes to his descendants. Thus, we would not expect the frequencies of the blood group genes to change appreciably in successive generations. We may recall that selection operates only when an individual is affected in such a way that, compared with those of other genotypes, he cannot contribute proportionately to the gene content of the population in the following generation.

SUGGESTIONS FOR FURTHER READING

ALLISON, A. C. 1956. Sickle cells and evolution. *Scientific American,* August, pp. 87–94.

ANFINSEN, C. B. 1963. *The molecular basis of evolution.* New York: John Wiley & Sons, Inc.

CLARKE, C. A. 1968. The prevention of "Rhesus" babies. *Scientific American,* November, pp. 46–52.

DOBZHANSKY, T. 1962. *Mankind evolving.* New Haven: Yale University Press.

GRAY, G. W. 1951. Sickle-cell anemia. *Scientific American,* August, pp. 56–59.

INGRAM, V. M. 1958. How do genes act? *Scientific American,* January, pp. 68–74.

SHEPPARD, P. M. 1959. *Natural selection and heredity.* New York: Philosophical Library, Inc.

8 Nonadaptive Evolution

The peculiar multilegged condition of the bullfrog (see again Fig. 1.1) is a rarity in nature. Yet we witnessed in a particular locality in 1958 an exceptionally high incidence of this defective trait. We have surmised that the deformity is caused by a recessive mutant gene. Since harmful recessive genes in a population tend to be carried mostly in the heterozygous state, the multilegged frogs probably arose from matings of heterozygous carriers. The probability of two or more carriers actually meeting is obviously greater in a small population than in a large breeding assemblage. Populations, of course, do fluctuate in size from time to time. It is not unthinkable that an unduly harsh winter sharply reduced the size of our particular bullfrog population. By sheer chance, an unusually large proportion of heterozygous carriers of the multilegged trait might have survived the winter's severity and prevailed as parents in the ensuing spring's breeding aggregation. In this manner, the "multilegged" gene, although not at all advantageous, would occur with uncommonly high frequency in the new generation of offspring. Such a fortuitous change in the genetic makeup of a population that may arise when the population becomes restricted in size is known as *genetic drift*.

ROLE OF GENETIC DRIFT

An examination of another situation in nature that may be illustrative of genetic drift will lead us into a simplified mathematical consideration of the concept. Coleman Goin, a naturalist at the University of Florida, studied the distribution of pigment variants of a terrestrial frog, known impressively as *Eleutherodactylus ricordi planirostris*. The frog will be referred to simply by its vernacular name, the greenhouse frog. This frog may possess either of two pigmentary patterns, mottled or striped (Fig.

8.1). A unique feature of the greenhouse frog is the terrestrial development of its eggs. That is to say, the eggs need not be submerged completely
in water, but can develop in moist earth. This important quality may
have considerable bearing on the dispersal of the frogs. Goin reared eggs
successfully in a flowerpot two-thirds filled with beach sand and placed in
a finger bowl of water. An examination of a large number of progency
hatched from many different clutches of eggs revealed that the striped
pattern is dominant to the mottled pattern.

The greenhouse frog is widespread in Cuba and the Bahama Islands,
and has only recently become established in Florida. Cuba apparently
has been the center of dispersal from which the Florida populations have
been derived. The present distribution of the greenhouse frog in Florida

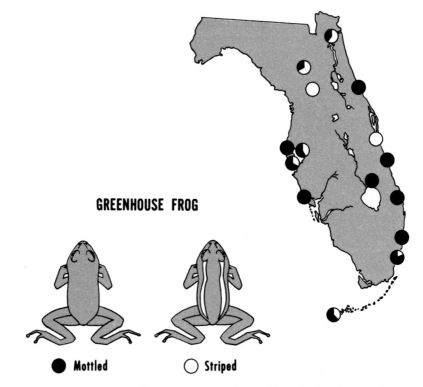

GREENHOUSE FROG

● Mottled   ○ Striped

FIG. 8.1. Distribution of the greenhouse frog in Florida, and the
relative frequencies of the two pattern variants, mottled and striped. The
populations are small and isolated, and differ appreciably in the incidences of mottled and striped forms. The varied frequencies may not be
due to natural selection, but may represent the outcome of chance fluctuations of genes, or genetic drift. (Based on studies by Coleman Goin.)

consists of a series of small, isolated colonies. As shown in Figure 8.1, the proportions of the two patterns vary in different colonies in Florida. In several colonies, only the mottled type occurs. What can account for the local preponderance of one or the other pattern, or even the absence of one of the contrasting patterns?

Goin conjectures that the greenhouse frog was introduced into Florida by means of clutches of eggs accidentally included in shipments of plants from Cuba, a distinct possibility in view of the terrestrial development of the eggs. Thus, a single clutch of introduced eggs could initiate a small colony, which, in turn, would establish at the outset a given pattern or proportion of patterns. The presence of only mottled forms in a population may be due to the chance circumstance that only mottled eggs were introduced. Or, perhaps both striped and mottled eggs were included in the shipment, but by sheer accident, one type was lost in succeeding generations.

It should be understood that Goin has not proved that the unusual distribution and frequency of the two pigment patterns are due solely to chance. Genetic drift is, however, a reasonable explanation.

THEORY OF GENETIC DRIFT

The theory of genetic drift was systematically developed in the 1930's by the geneticist Sewall Wright, then at the University of Chicago and later at the University of Wisconsin. In fact, the phenomenon of drift is frequently called the "Sewall Wright effect." The following modest mathematical treatment will reveal the essential features of the process.

Let us assume that the numerous isolated colonies in Florida were each settled by only two frogs, a male and a female, both of constitutions Aa. Let us further suppose that each mated pair produces only two offspring. The possible genotypes of the progeny, and the chance associations of the genotypes, are shown in Table 8.1.

Several meaningful considerations emerge from Table 8.1. For example, the chance that the first offspring from a cross of two heterozygous parents will be AA is $\frac{1}{4}$. The second event is independent of the first; hence, the chance that the second offspring will be AA is also $\frac{1}{4}$. The chance that *both* offspring will be AA is the product of the separate probabilities of the two independent events, $\frac{1}{4} \times \frac{1}{4}$, or $\frac{1}{16}$.

We may now ask: What is the probability of producing two offspring, one AA and the other Aa, *in no particular order?* From Table 8.1, it may be seen that the chance of obtaining an AA individual followed by an Aa individual is $\frac{2}{16}$. Now, the wording of our question requires that we consider a second possibility, that of an Aa offspring followed by an AA offspring (also $\frac{2}{16}$). These two probabilities must be added together to arrive at the chance of producing the two genotypes irrespective of the order of birth. Hence, in the case in question, the chance is $\frac{2}{16} + \frac{2}{16}$, or $\frac{4}{16}$. In like manner, it may be ascertained that the expectation of obtaining one *AA* and one *aa* offspring (in no given order) is $\frac{2}{16}$; and that of producing one *Aa* and one *aa* (in any sequence) is $\frac{4}{16}$.

The essential point is that any one of the above circumstances may occur in a given colony. We may concentrate on one situation. The probability that a colony will have only two *AA* offspring is 1 in 16. Thus, by the simple play of chance, the parents initiating the colony might not leave an *aa* offspring. The *a* gene would be immediately lost in the population. Subsequent generations descended from the first-generation *AA* individuals would contain, barring mutation, only *AA* types. Chance alone can there-

TABLE 8.1   *Chance Distribution of Offspring of Two Heterozygous Parents* (Aa × Aa)

Genotype of first offspring	Probability of first event	Genotype of second offspring	Probability of second event	Total Probability
AA	$\frac{1}{4}$	*AA*	$\frac{1}{4}$	both offspring *AA*, $\frac{1}{16}$
AA	$\frac{1}{4}$	*Aa*	$\frac{2}{4}$	*AA* followed by *Aa*, $\frac{2}{16}$
AA	$\frac{1}{4}$	*aa*	$\frac{1}{4}$	*AA* followed by *aa*, $\frac{1}{16}$
Aa	$\frac{2}{4}$	*AA*	$\frac{1}{4}$	*Aa* followed by *AA*, $\frac{2}{16}$
Aa	$\frac{2}{4}$	*Aa*	$\frac{2}{4}$	both offspring *Aa*, $\frac{4}{16}$
Aa	$\frac{2}{4}$	*aa*	$\frac{1}{4}$	*Aa* followed by *aa*, $\frac{2}{16}$
aa	$\frac{1}{4}$	*AA*	$\frac{1}{4}$	*aa* followed by *AA*, $\frac{1}{16}$
aa	$\frac{1}{4}$	*Aa*	$\frac{2}{4}$	*aa* followed by *Aa*, $\frac{2}{16}$
aa	$\frac{1}{4}$	*aa*	$\frac{1}{4}$	both offspring *aa*, $\frac{1}{16}$

fore lead to an irreversible situation. A gene once lost could not readily establish itself again in the population. The decisive factor is the size of the population. When populations are small, striking changes can occur from one generation to the next. Some genes may be lost or reduced in frequency by sheer chance; others may be accidentally increased in frequency. Thus, the genetic architecture of a small population may change irrespective of the selective advantage or disadvantage of a trait. Indeed, a beneficial gene may be lost in a small population before it has had the opportunity to be acted upon favorably by natural selection. Evolution in this case is *nonadaptive*.

FOUNDER PRINCIPLE

When a few individuals or a small group migrate from a main population, only a limited portion of the parental gene pool is carried away. In the small migrant group, some genes may be perchance absent or in such low frequency that they may be easily lost. The fortuitous changes in the gene frequencies of newly founded populations has been called the *founder principle*. This term simply signifies a special case of genetic drift.

The American Indians afford a possible example of the loss of genes by the founder principle. North American Indian tribes, for the most part, surprisingly have no I^B genes that govern type B blood. However, in Asia, the ancestral home of the American Indian, the I^B gene is widespread. The ancestral population of Mongoloids that migrated across the Bering Strait to North America might well have been very small. Accordingly, the possibility exists that none of the prehistoric immigrants happened to be of blood group B. It is also conceivable that a few individuals of the migrant band did carry the I^B gene, but they perchance failed to leave descendants.

The interpretation based on genetic drift should not be considered as definitive. The operation of natural selection cannot be flatly dismissed (see chapter 7). Most of the North American Indians possess only blood group O, or, stated another way, contain only the blood group allele, *i*. With few exceptions, the North American Indian tribes have lost not only blood group allele I^B but gene I^A as well. The loss of both alleles, I^A and I^B, by sheer chance perhaps defies credibility. Indeed, many modern students of evolution are convinced that some strong selective force led to the rapid elimination of the I^A and I^B genes in the American Indian populations. If this is true, it would offer an impressive example of the action of natural selection in modifying the frequencies of genes in a population.

RELIGIOUS ISOLATES

The most likely situation to witness the phenomenon of genetic drift is one in which the population is virtually a small, self-contained breeding unit, or *isolate*, in the midst of a larger population. This typifies the Dunkers, a very small religious sect in eastern Pennsylvania. The Dunkers are descendants of the Old German Baptist Brethren, who came to the United States in the early eighteenth century. Bentley Glass of Johns Hopkins University has studied the community of Dunkers in Franklin County, Pennsylvania, which numbers about 300 individuals. In each generation, the number of parents has remained stable at about 90. The Dunkers live on farms intermingled with the general population, but are genetically isolated by rigid marriage customs. The choice of mates is restricted to members within the religious group.

Glass, with his colleagues, compared the frequencies of certain traits in the Dunker Community with those of the surrounding heterogeneous American population and with those of the population in western Germany from which the Dunker sect had emigrated two centuries ago. Such a comparison of a small isolate with its large host and parent populations should reveal the effectiveness, if any, of genetic drift. Analyses were made of the patterns of inheritance of three blood group systems—the ABO blood groups, the MN blood types, and the Rh blood types. In addition, data were accumulated on the incidences of four external traits; namely, the configuration of the ear lobes (which either may be attached to the side of the head or hang free), right- or left-handedness, the presence or absence of hair on the middle segments of the fingers ("mid-digital hair"), and "hitch-hiker's thumb," technically termed *distal hyperextensibility* (Fig. 8.2).

The frequencies of many of these traits are strikingly different in the Dunker community from those of the general United States and West Germany populations. Blood group A is much more frequent among the Dunkers; the O group is somewhat rarer in the Dunkers; and the frequencies of groups B and AB have dropped to exceptionally low levels in the Dunker community. In fact, the I^B gene had almost been lost in the isolate. Most of the carriers of the I^B gene were not born in the community, but were converts who entered the isolate by marriage.

A noticeable change has also occurred in the incidences of the M and N blood types in the Dunker community. Type M has increased in frequency, and type N has dwindled in frequency as compared with the incidences of these blood types in either the general United States population or the West Germany population. Only the Rh blood groups do the Dunkers conform closely to their surrounding large population.

With respect to physical traits, equally striking differences were found. Briefly, the frequencies of mid-digital hair patterns, distal hyperextensibility of the thumb, and attached ear lobes are significantly lower in the Dunker isolate than in the surrounding American populations. The Dunkers do, however, agree well with other large populations in the incidence of lefthandedness. It would thus appear that the peculiar constellation of gene frequencies in the Dunker community—some uncommonly high, others uniquely low, and still others, unchanged from the general large population—can be best attributed to chance fluctuations, or genetic drift.

There is no concurrence of opinion among evolutionists concerning the operation of genetic drift in natural populations, but few would deny that small religious isolates have felt the effect of random sampling. It should be clear, however, that genetic drift becomes ineffectual when a

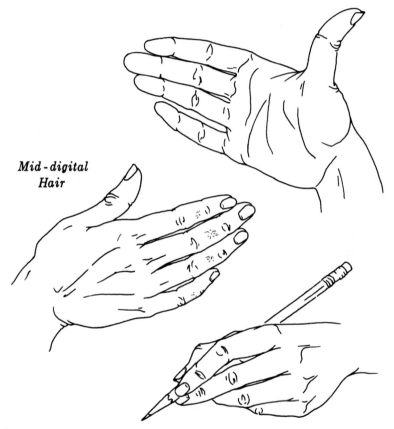

Attached Lobe   *Free Lobe*   *Hyperextensibility of Thumb*

Mid-digital Hair

Left-handedness

Fig. 8.2. Inheritable physical traits—nature of ear lobes, "hitch-hiker's thumb," mid-digital hair, and handedness—studied by Bentley Glass and his co-workers in members of the small religious community of Dunkers in Pennsylvania. The distinctive frequencies of most of these traits in the Dunker population suggest the operation of genetic drift.

small community increases in size. Fluctuations or shifts in gene frequencies in large populations are determined almost exclusively by selection.

GENE FLOW

A rich archaeological record reveals considerable movement on the part of early human populations. Some migrations were sporadic, in small groups; others were more or less continual streams, involving large numbers of peoples. Large-scale immigrations followed by interbreeding have the effect of introducing new genes to the host populations. The diffusion of genes into populations through migrations is referred to by geneticists as *gene flow*.

The graded distribution of the I^B blood-group gene in Europe represents the historical consequence of invasions by Mongolians who pushed westward repeatedly between the sixth and sixteenth centuries (Fig. 8.3). There is a high frequency of the I^B gene in central Asia. In Europe, the frequency of the I^B gene diminishes steadily from the borders of Asia to a

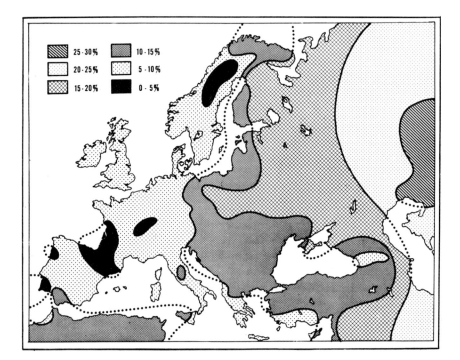

FIG. 8.3. Gradient of frequencies of the I^B blood-group gene from central Asia to western Europe. (Based on studies by A. E. Mourant.)

low level of 5 percent or less in parts of Holland, France, Spain, and Portugal. The Basque peoples, who inhabit the region of the Pyrenees in Spain and France, have the lowest frequency of the I^B gene—below 3 percent—in Europe. From a biological standpoint, the Basque community of long standing is a cohesive, endogamous mating unit. The exceptionally low incidence of the I^B gene among the Basques may be taken to indicate that there has been little intermarriage with surrounding populations. It is possible that a few centuries ago the I^B gene was completely absent from the self-contained Basque community.

The exchange of genes between populations may have dramatic consequences. Until recently, hemolytic disease of the newborn, or Rh disease, was virtually unknown in China. All Chinese women are Rh-positive (RR). However, intermarriage between immigrant Americans and the native Chinese has led to the introduction of the Rh-negative gene (r) in the Chinese population. No Rh disease would be witnessed in the immediate offspring of American men and Chinese women. Conversely, all marriages of Rh-negative American women (rr) and Rh-positive men (RR) would be of the incompatible type. All children by Chinese fathers would be Rh-positive (Rr) and potential victims of hemolytic disease.

Whereas American immigrants introduce the Rh-negative gene (r) into Chinese populations where it formerly was not present, Chinese immigrants (all of whom are RR) introduce more Rh-positive genes (R) into the American populations, thus diluting the Rh-negative gene pool in the United States. Initially the Rh-positive Chinese men (RR) married to Rh-negative American women (rr) would result in an increased incidence of Rh-diseased infants. In later generations, however, the frequency of Rh-negative women in the United States would be lower, inasmuch as women of mixed Chinese-American origin would be either RR or Rr, predominantly the former. Thus, in the United States, the long-range effect of Chinese-American intermarriage is a reduction in the incidence of hemolytic disease of the newborn.

SUGGESTIONS FOR FURTHER READING

DUNN, L. C. 1966. *Heredity and evolution in human populations.* New York: Atheneum.

DUNN, L. C. and DUNN, S. P. 1957. The Jewish community of Rome. *Scientific American*, March, pp. 118–128.

GLASS, B. 1953. The genetics of the Dunkers. *Scientific American*, August, pp. 76–81.

9 Races and Species

Any large assemblage of a particular organism is generally not distributed equally or uniformly throughout its territory or range in nature. A widespread group of plants or animals is typically subdivided into numerous local populations, each physically separated from the others to some extent. The environmental conditions in different parts of the range of an organism are not likely to be identical. We may thus expect that a given local population will consist of genetic types that are adapted to a specific set of prevailing environmental conditions. The degree to which each population maintains its genetic distinctness is governed by the extent to which interbreeding between the populations occurs. A free interchange of genes between populations will, of course, tend to blur the differences between the populations. But what are the consequences when gene exchange between populations is greatly restricted or prevented? This chapter addresses itself to this question.

VARIATION BETWEEN POPULATIONS

Our first consideration is to demonstrate that inheritable variations do indeed exist among the various breeding populations in different parts of the range of an organism. Jens Clausen, David Keck, and William Hiesey of the Carnegie Institution of Washington at Stanford, California, have shown that populations of the yarrow plant, *Achillea lanulosa*, from different parts of California are each adapted to their respective habitats. As revealed in Figure 9.1, the variations in height of the plant are correlated with altitudinal differences. The shortest plants are from the highest altitudes, and the plants increase in height in a gradient fashion with decreasing altitude. The term *cline*, or character gradient, has been applied to such situations where a character varies more or less continuously with a gradual change in the environmental terrain.

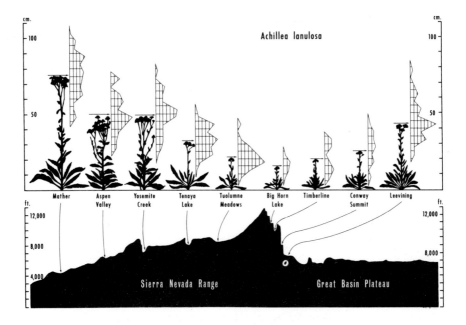

FIG. 9.1. Clinal variation in the yarrow plant, *Achillea lanulosa*. The increase in height of the plant is more or less continuous with decreasing altitude. The plants shown here are representatives from different populations in the Sierra Nevada Mountains of California that were grown in a uniform garden at Stanford, California. Each plant illustrated is one of average height for the given population; the graph adjacent to the plant reveals the distribution of heights within the population. (From Clausen, Keck, and Hiesey, *Carnegie Institution of Washington Publication 581*, 1948.)

The observation by itself that the yarrow plants are phenotypically dissimilar at different elevations does not indicate that they are genetically different. If the claim is to be made that the observed variations represent local adaptations resulting from the action of natural selection, then the hereditary basis for the differences in height should be demonstrated. It is often difficult to obtain data disclosing the hereditary nature of population differences. In this respect, the studies of Clausen and his co-workers are commendable. The plants shown in Figure 9.1 had actually been grown together in a uniform experimental garden at Stanford, California. The plants transplanted from various localities developed differently from one another in the same experimental garden, revealing that each population had evolved its own distinctive complex of genes.

RACES

The variation pattern in organisms may be discrete or discontinuous, particularly when the populations are separated from each other by pronounced physical barriers. This is exemplified by the varieties of the carpenter bee (*Xylocopa nobilis*) in the Celebes and neighboring islands of Indonesia (Fig. 9.2). As revealed by the studies of J. van der Vecht of the Museum of Natural History at Leiden, Netherlands, there are three different varieties on the mainland of Celebes, and at least three kinds on the adjacent small islands. These geographical variants differ conspicuously in the coloration of the small, soft hairs that cover the surface of the body. The first abdominal segment is invariably clothed with bright yellow hairs. However, each variety has evolved a unique constellation of colors on the other abdominal segments as well as on the thorax.

The variations in the carpenter bees within and between islands are well defined and easily distinguishable. One may refer to populations with well-marked discontinuities as *races*. Races are simply geographical aggregates of populations that differ in the incidence of genetic traits. How genetically different two assemblages of populations must be to warrant racial designations is an open question.

Some of the problems inherent in the delimitation of races are exemplified by the different temperature-adapted populations of the North American leopard frog, *Rana pipiens*. John A. Moore, then at Columbia University and later at the University of California, has tested the effects of temperature on the development of the embryos of frogs from widely different localities in order to ascertain the endurable limits of tolerance of the embryos. The major findings are shown in Table 9.1.

It may be seen that embryos of northern populations are more resistant to low temperatures and less tolerant of high temperatures than are embryos from southern populations. Embryos of populations from Quebec, Vermont, Wisconsin, and New Jersey have approximately the same range of temperature tolerances. Some of these northern embryos for which data are available can resist temperatures as low as 5°C. Embryos from Louisiana, Florida, Texas, and Mexico differ markedly from those of northern populations. These southerly distributed embryos can tolerate high temperatures—some as high as 35°C—but are very susceptible to low temperatures. Hence, northern and southern populations have become adapted to different environments in their respective territories.

We may refer to the northern populations as the cold-adapted race of the leopard frog, and designate the southern populations as the warm-adapted race. It is, of course, evident that we are being arbitrary in drawing a fine line of demarcation between northern and southern races. Data

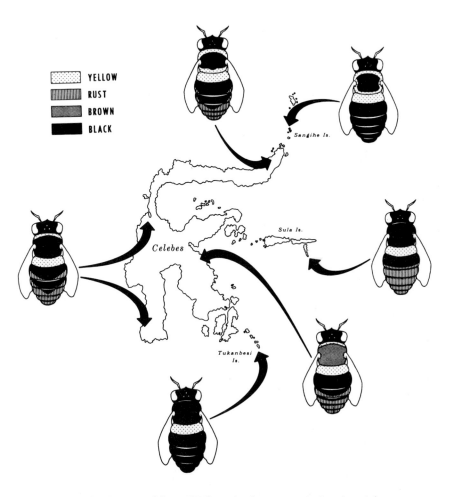

FIG. 9.2. Geographic variation of color pattern in females of the carpenter bee, *Xylocopa nobilis*, in the Celebes and neighboring islands in Indonesia. Each geographic race has evolved a distinctive constellation of colors. (Based on studies by J. van der Vecht.)

TABLE 9.1 *Limits of Temperature Tolerance of Embryos of the North American Leopard Frog,* Rana pipiens

Locality and Latitude	Lower Limiting Temperature (°C)	Upper Limiting Temperature (°C)
Quebec, 46°N	No data	28
Vermont, 45°N	5	28
Wisconsin, 44°N	No data	28
New Jersey, 40°N	5	28
Louisiana, 30°N	5	32
Northern Florida, 29°N	9	33
Southern Florida, 27°N	11	35
Texas, 32°N	10	32
Eastern Mexico, 22°N	12	33

are presently lacking for the geographically intermediate populations, but further studies will probably reveal that the temperature adaptations of the frog embryos change gradually north to south. Even with the present information, one may wish to recognize more than two temperature-adapted races, or perhaps, as some investigators firmly argue, refrain completely from making racial designations.

Races may be best thought of as units of organization below the species level. In other words, races may be considered as stages in the transformation of populations into species. But what constitutes a species? Up to this point we have assiduously avoided the use of the term *species*. A discussion of the process leading to the formation of species will facilitate understanding of the term itself.

FORMATION OF SPECIES

Let us imagine a large assemblage of land snails subdivided in three geographical aggregations or races, A, B, and C, each adapted to local environmental conditions (Fig. 9.3). There are initially no gross barriers separating the populations from each other, and where A meets B and B meets C, interbreeding occurs. Zones of intermediate individuals are thus established between the races, and the width of these zones depends upon the extent to which the respective populations intermingle. It is important to realize that races are fully capable of exchanging genes with one another.

We may now visualize (Fig. 9.3) some striking physical feature, such as a great river, forging its way through the territory and effectively isolating the land snails of race C from those of B. These two assemblages may be spatially separated from each other for an indefinitely long period of time, affording an opportunity for race C to pursue its own independent evolutionary course. Two populations that are geographically separated, like B and C in our pictorial model, are said to be *allopatric*. (Technically speaking, A and B are also allopatric, since they, for the most part, occupy different geographical areas.)

After eons of time, the river may dry up and the hollow bed may eventually become filled in with land. Now, if the members of populations B and C were to extend their ranges and meet again, one of two things might happen. The snails of the two populations may freely interbreed and establish once again a zone of intermediate individuals. On the other hand, the two populations may no longer be able to interchange genes. If the two assemblages can exist side by side without interbreeding, then the two groups have reached the evolutionary status of separate species. *A species is a breeding community that preserves its genetic identity by its inability to exchange genes with other such breeding communities.* In our pictorial model (Fig. 9.3), race C has become transformed into a new species, C'. Two species (A-B and C') have now arisen where formerly only one existed. It should be noted that races A and B are treated as members of a single species since no barriers to gene exchange exist between them.

NOMENCLATURE

The scientific names that the taxonomist would apply to our populations of land snails deserve special comment. The technical name of a species consists of two words, in Latin or in latinized form. An acceptable designation of the original species of land snails depicted in Figure 9.3 would be *Helix typicus*. The first word is the name of a comprehensive group, the genus, to which land snails belong; the second word is a name unique to the species. The taxonomist would be obliged to create a different latinized second name for the newly derived species of land snail, the C' population in Figure 9.3. This new species might well be called *Helix varians*. The name of the genus remains the same since the two species are closely related. The genus, therefore, denotes a group of interrelated species.

The binomial ("two-named") system of nomenclature, universally accepted, was devised by the Swedish naturalist Linnaeus (born Carl von Linné) in his monumental work, *Systema Naturae*, first published in 1735. Convention dictates that the first letter of the generic name be capitalized and that the specific name begin with a small letter. It is also customary to print the scientific name of a species in italics, or in a type that is different from that of the accompanying text. A modern refinement of the Linnaean system is the introduction of a third italicized name, which signifies the subspecies. Geographical races are recognized taxonomically as subspecies. Thus, it would be appropriate to designate races A and B (Fig.

Geographical Variation

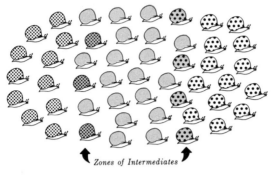
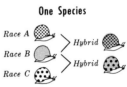

One Species

Race A ⟩ Hybrid
Race B
Race C ⟩ Hybrid

Zones of Intermediates

Isolating Action of Geographic Barrier

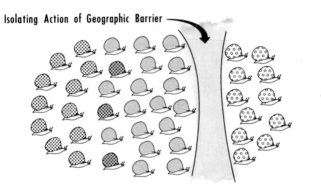

$C \longrightarrow C'$

Removal of Geographic Barrier

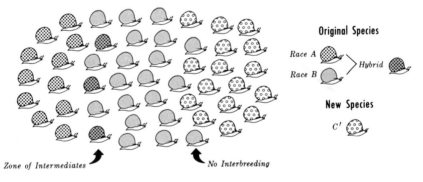

Original Species

Race A ⟩ Hybrid
Race B

New Species

C'

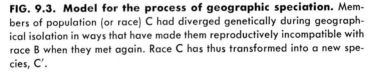

Zone of Intermediates   *No Interbreeding*

FIG. 9.3. Model for the process of geographic speciation. Members of population (or race) C had diverged genetically during geographical isolation in ways that have made them reproductively incompatible with race B when they met again. Race C has thus transformed into a new species, C'.

9.3) as *Helix typicus elegans* and *Helix typicus eminens*, respectively. Such a species composed of two (or more) subspecies is said to be polytypic. A monotypic species is one that is not differentiated into two or more geographical races or subspecies, like *Helix varians*.

REPRODUCTIVE ISOLATING MECHANISMS

We have seen that two populations (or races), while spatially separated from each other, may accumulate sufficient genetic differences in isolation that they would no longer be able to interchange genes if and when they came into contact with one another. When the geographical barrier persists, it is difficult to judge the extent to which the two allopatric populations have diverged genetically from each other. Only when the two populations come together again does it become apparent whether or not they have changed in ways that would make them reproductively incompatible. Two populations that come to occupy the same territory are called *sympatric*. The ways or agencies that prevent interbreeding between sympatric species are known as *reproductive isolating mechanisms*.

Reproductive isolating mechanisms take varied forms, and one or more of the different types may be found separating two species. The major isolating mechanisms can be enumerated as follows:

1. Ecological or habitat isolation
2. Seasonal or temporal isolation
3. Sexual or ethological isolation
4. Mechanical isolation
5. Gametic isolation
6. Hybrid inviability
7. Hybrid sterility

Each of these kinds may be illustrated by considering again the two species of land snails. The two groups may live in the same general area, but actually occupy different ecological niches. One may prefer a moist soil; the other may select a drier habitat. They are thus effectively separated by different *ecological* or *habitat* preferences. The two species may also retain their distinctness by breeding at different times of the year (*seasonal isolation*). The breeding seasons may overlap, but interbreeding may not occur because of the lack of mutual attraction between the sexes of the two species (*sexual isolation*). If the two land species do mingle, it is possible that the external sexual apparatus of one species is physically incompatible with the genitalia of the other species (*mechanical isolation*).

The male of one species may inseminate the female of the other, but the sperm cells may be inviable in the reproductive tract of the female. This form of *gametic isolation* is not unique to animals; in plants, such as the Jimson weed (Datura), the pollen tubes of one species are unable to grow in the styles of other species.

Cross-fertilizations between two species may be successful, but the hybrid embryos may be abnormal or fail to reach sexual maturity (*hybrid inviability*). For example, two species of the chicory plant, *Crepis tectorum* and *Crepis capillaris*, can be crossed, but the hybrid seedlings die in early development. Crosses between the bullfrog, *Rana catesbeiana*, and the green frog, *Rana clamitans*, result in inviable embryos. In certain hybrid crosses, such as between females of the toad species *Bufo fowleri* and males of *Bufo valliceps*, the hybrids may survive but are completely sterile (*hybrid sterility*). The familiar example of hybrid sterility is the mule, the offspring of a male ass and a mare.

In essence, two populations can remain genetically distinct, and be designated as species, when gene exchange between them is prevented or limited by one or more reproductive isolating mechanisms. More often than not, we are unable to obtain direct evidence for the presence or absence of interbreeding in nature between two groups. The degree of reproductive isolation is then indirectly gauged by the extent to which the members of two populations differ in morphological, physiological, and behavioral characteristics. Two populations that are morphologically very dissimilar are likely to be distinct species. It should be understood, however, that the level of morphological differentiation cannot be used with implicit confidence as a criterion of a species. For example, two species of fruit flies, *Drosophila pseudoobscura* and *Drosophila persimilis*, are reproductively isolated, but are almost indistinguishable on morphological grounds.

ORIGIN OF ISOLATING MECHANISMS

How do reproductive isolating mechanisms arise? In the 1940's, a series of instructive evolutionary studies on the leopard frog, *Rana pipiens*, was undertaken by John A. Moore. The leopard frog is widely distributed in North America, ranging from northern Canada through the United States and Mexico into the lower reaches of Central America. Moore obtained leopard frogs from different geographical populations and crossed them in the laboratory. When frogs from northeastern United States (Vermont) were crossed with their southerly distributed lowland relatives in eastern Mexico (Axtla in San Luis Potosi), the hybrid embryos failed to develop normally. Thus, the geographically extreme members of this species have diverged genetically to the extent that they are incapable of producing viable hybrids in the laboratory.

It must be admitted that the possibility of a Vermont frog crossing with a Mexican frog in nature is extremely remote. It took a biologist to bring these two frogs together. Yet it is just this point which emphasizes the fact that an isolating mechanism, such as hybrid inviability, does not develop for the effect itself, but is simply the natural consequence of two populations accumulating sufficient genetic differences during a long period of geographical separation. Hermann J. Muller of Indiana University was among the first to advance the concept that isolating mechanisms originate as a by-product of genetic divergence of allopatric populations. The genetic changes which arise to better adapt one population to particular environmental conditions may also be instrumental in reproductively isolating that population from other populations which possess different adaptive gene complexes. We had seen earlier that the embryos of Vermont leopard frogs differ considerably in their range of temperature tolerance from embryos of eastern Mexican frogs (Table 9.1). It might well be, then, that the embryonic defects in hybrids between these northern and southern frogs are associated with the different temperature adaptations of the parental eggs.

If the Vermont and Mexican leopard frogs were ever to meet in nature, then any intercrosses between them would lead to the formation of inviable hybrids. This would represent a wastage of reproductive energy of the parental frogs. Theodosius Dobzhansky has advanced the interesting hypothesis that, under such conditions, natural selection would promote the establishment of isolating mechanisms which would guard against the production of abnormal hybrids. In frogs, a normal mating or a mismating in a mixed population depends principally upon the discrimination of the female. The reproductive potential of an undiscriminating female is obviously lower than that of a female who leaves normal offspring. If the tendency to mismate is inheritable, then the genes responsible for this tendency will eventually be lost or sharply reduced in frequency by virtue of the elimination of the indiscriminate females, an elimination effectively accomplished by the inviability of their offspring. Thus, the continual propagation of females that most resist the attentions of "foreign" males will lead eventually to a situation in which mismatings do not occur, and abnormal hybrids are not produced at all.

Karl Koopman, an able student of Theodosius Dobzhansky, has tested the hypothesis that natural selection tends to strengthen, or make complete, the reproductive isolation between two species coexisting in the same territory. Koopman used for experimentation two species of fruit flies, *Drosophila pseudoobscura* and *Drosophila persimilis*. In nature, sexual selection between these two sympatric species is strong, and interspecific matings do not occur. However, in a mixed population in the laboratory, particularly at low temperatures, mismatings do take place. Koopman accordingly brought together members of both species in an experimental cage and purposely kept the cage at a low temperature (16°C). Hybrid flies were produced and were viable, but Koopman in effect made them inviable by painstakingly removing them from the breeding cage when each new generation emerged. Over a period of several generations the production of hybrid flies dwindled markedly and mismatings in the population cage were substantially curtailed. This is a dramatic demonstration of the efficacy of selection in strengthening reproductive isolation between two sympatric species.

MAN: A SINGLE VARIABLE SPECIES

There is only one present-day species of man, *Homo sapiens*. Different populations of man can interbreed successfully, and, in fact, do. The extensive commingling of populations renders it difficult, if not impossible, to establish discrete racial categories in man. Races, as we have seen, are geographically defined aggregates of local populations. The populations of mankind are not sharply separated geographically from one another. Multiple migrations of peoples and innumerable intermarriages have tended to blur the genetical contrasts between populations. The boundaries of human races, if they can be delimited at all, are at best fuzzy, ever-shifting with time. The diversity and distribution of mankind is shown in Figure 9.4. Man can be classified as having three great divisions, the Caucasoid, the Mongoloid, and the Negroid.

The term *race* is regrettably one of the most abused words in the vocabulary of unenlightened persons. It is exceedingly important to recognize that a race is *not* a community based on language, literature, religion, nationality, or customs. There are Aryan languages, but there is not an Aryan race. Aryans are peoples of diverse genetical makeups who speak a common tongue (Indo-European). *Aryan* is therefore nothing more than a linguistic designation. In like manner, there is a Jewish religion, but not a Jewish race. And there is an Italian nation, but not an Italian race. A race is a reproductive community of individuals occupying a definite region, and in one and the same geographical region may be found Aryans, Jews, and Italians. Every human population today consists of a multitude of diverse genotypes. A "pure" population or race, in which all members are genetically alike, is a myth and a blatant absurdity.

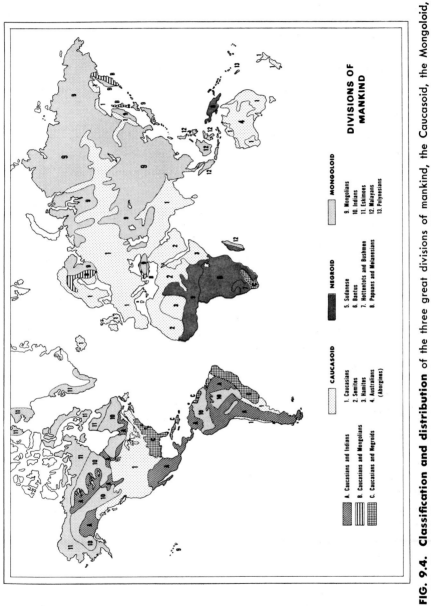

FIG. 9.4. Classification and distribution of the three great divisions of mankind, the Caucasoid, the Mongoloid, and the Negroid. These three principal groups have numerous subgroups within them.

SUGGESTIONS FOR FURTHER READING

DOBZHANSKY, T. 1951. *Genetics and the origin of species.* New York: Columbia University Press.

DOWDESWELL, W. H. 1960. *The mechanism of evolution.* New York: Harper & Row, Publishers.

GRANT, V. 1963. *The origin of adaptations.* New York: Columbia University Press.

MAYR, E. 1942. *Systematics and the origin of species.* New York: Columbia University Press.

MERRELL, D. J. 1962. *Evolution and genetics.* New York: Holt, Rinehart & Winston, Inc.

MOODY, P. A. 1962. *Introduction to evolution.* New York: Harper & Row, Publishers.

SIMPSON, G. G. 1953. *The major features of evolution.* New York: Columbia University Press.

STEBBINS, G. L. 1966. *Processes of organic evolution.* Englewood Cliffs, N.J.: Prentice-Hall, Inc.

10 Cataclysmic Evolution

The process leading to the formation of a new species generally extends over a great reach of time. As we have seen, the origin of new species involves a long period of geographical isolation and the long-term influences of natural selection. A sudden and rapid emergence of a new kind of organism is scarcely imaginable. Yet a natural mechanism does exist whereby a new species can arise rather abruptly. The process is associated with the phenomenon of *polyploidy*, or the multiplication of the chromosome complement of an organism. Species formation through polyploidy has occurred almost entirely, if not exclusively, in the plant kingdom. Many of our valuable cultivated crop plants, such as wheat, oats, cotton, tobacco, and sugar cane trace their origin to this cataclysmic or explosive type of evolution.

WHEAT

The domestic wheats and their wild relatives have an intriguing evolutionary history. There are numerous species of wheat, all of which fall into three major categories on the basis of their chromosome numbers. The most ancient type is the small-grain einkorn wheat, containing 14 chromosomes in its body (somatic) cells. There are two species, one wild and the other cultivated, both of which may be found growing in the hilly regions of southeastern Europe and southwestern Asia. Cultivated einkorn has slightly larger kernels than the wild form, but the yields of each are low and the grain is used principally for feeding cattle and horses.

Another assemblage of wheat, once widely grown, is the emmer series of which there are at least six species. The chromosome number in the nuclei of somatic cells of emmer wheats is 28. These varieties, found in Europe and the United States, are used today principally as stock feed, although one of them, called durum wheat, is of commercial value in the production of macaroni and spaghetti.

The most recently evolved, and by far the most valuable agriculturally, are the bread wheats. The bread wheats have not been known to occur in the wild state; all are cultivated types. The bread wheats have 42 chromosomes. These wheats, high in protein content, comprise almost 90 percent of all the wheat harvested in the world today.

The various species of wheats thus fall into three major groups, with 14, 28, and 42 chromosomes, respectively. A list of the representatives of these three groups is given in Table 10.1.

TABLE 10.1   *Species of Wheat* (Triticum)

14 Chromosomes	28 Chromosomes	42 Chromosomes
T. aegilopoides (wild einkorn)	*T. dicoccoides* (wild emmer)	*T. aestivum* (bread wheat)
T. monococcum (cultivated einkorn)	*T. dicoccum* (cultivated emmer)	*T. sphaerococcum* (shot wheat)
	T. durum (macaroni wheat)	*T. compactum* (club wheat)
	T. persicum (persian wheat)	*T. spelta* (spelt)
	T. turgidum (rivet wheat)	*T. macha* (macha wheat)
	T. polonicum (polish wheat)	

ORIGIN OF WHEAT SPECIES

Virtually all authorities are agreed on the sequence of evolutionary events depicted in Figure 10.1. Einkorn wheat, possessing a chromosome number of 14, was doubtless one of the ancestral parents of the 28-chromosome emmer assemblage. A most remarkable, but generally accepted, thesis is that the other parent was not a wheat at all, but rather *Aegilops speltoides*, a wild grass with 14 chromosomes. This wild grass parent occurs as a common weed in the wheat fields of southwestern Asia. The cross of einkorn wheat and the wild grass would yield an F_1 hybrid that possesses 14 chromosomes, 7 from each parent. We may designate the 7 chromosomes from one parent species as set (or genome) *A*, and the 7 from the other parent species as set (or genome) *B*. Accordingly, the F_1 hybrids would have the *AB* genomes.

If the chromosome complement in the hybrid accidentally doubled, then the hybrid would contain 28 instead of 14 chromosomes and pass on the doubled set of chromosomes to its offspring. Such an event, strange as it may seem, accounts for the emergence of the 28-chromosome emmer wheat. This new species is characterized as having the *AABB* genomes.

In turn, the 28-chromosome emmer wheat was the ancestor of the 42-chromosome bread wheat. In the early 1900's, the British botanist John Percival hazarded the opinion that the bread wheat group arose by hybridization of a species of wheat of the emmer group (28 chromosomes) and goat grass, *Aegilops squarrosa*, a useless weed commonly found growing in wheat fields in the Mediterranean area. Although this startling suggestion was initially viewed with skepticism, it is currently conceded that Percival was correct. *Aegilops squarrosa* possesses 14 chromosomes, and thus would transmit 7 of its chromosomes (set *C*) to the hybrid. The hybrid would contain 21 chromosomes (sets *ABC*), having received 14 (sets *AB*) from its emmer wheat parent. The subsequent duplication in the hybrid of each chromosome set provided by the parents would result in a 42-chromosome wheat species (*AABBCC*).

The initial F_1 hybrid between einkorn wheat and *Aegilops speltoides* (or between emmer wheat and *Aegilops squarrosa*) is sterile, but when the chromosome complement doubles, then a fully fertile species arises. Is it to be expected that the F_1 hybrid would be sterile? And what would account for the fertility of the hybrid when chromosome doubling occurred? This requires a deeper look into the phenomenon of polyploidy, to which we shall now turn.

THE MECHANISM OF SPECIATION BY POLYPLOIDY

Figure 10.2 illustrates the underlying basis of the fertility of a formerly sterile hybrid resulting from the doubling of its chromosome number. For ease of presentation, the parental species are shown with a small number of chromosomes, 6 and 4 respectively. It should be noted that the chromosomes are present in pairs. The members of each pair are alike or homologous, but each pair is distinguishable from the other. Thus, the 6-chromosome parent possesses three different pairs of chromosomes; the 4-chromosome parent, two different pairs.

The gametes, egg cells and pollen cells (sperm), are derived by cell divisions of a special kind, called meiosis. One of the essential features of the process of meiosis is that the members of each pair are attracted to each other and come to lie side by side in the nucleus. The meiotic cell divisions are intricate, but the pertinent outcome is the separation of like, or homologous, chromosomes such that each gamete comes to possess only one member of each pair of chromosomes. Each gamete is said to contain

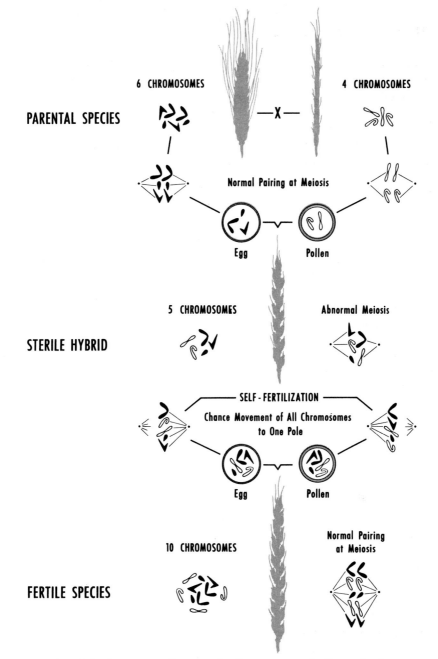

FIG. 10.2. Sequence of events leading to a new, fertile species from two old species by hybridization and polyploidy. The F₁ hybrid plant derived from a cross of the two parental species is sterile. The F₁ hybrid may occasionally produce viable gametes when all chromosomes fortuitously enter a gamete during the process of meiosis. The fusion of such gametes leads to a new form of plant, which contains two complete sets of chromosomes (one full set of each of the original parents).

a *haploid* complement of chromosomes, or half the number found in a somatic cell. The latter, in turn, is described as being *diploid* in chromosome number.

The sterility of the first-generation hybrid is now comprehensible. There are simply no homologous chromosomes in the F_1 hybrid. Each chromosome lacks a homologue to act as its pairing partner at meiosis. The process of meiosis in the hybrid is chaotic; the chromosomes move at random into the gametes. The eggs and pollen cells typically contain an odd assortment of chromosomes and are nonfunctional.

Occasionally, by sheer chance, a few gametes might be produced by the F_1 hybrid that contain all the chromosomes (Fig. 10.2). These gametes would be functional, and the fusion of such sex cells would give rise to a plant that contains twice the number of chromosomes that the first-generation hybrid possessed. The plant actually would contain two complete sets of chromosomes; that is, the full diploid complement of chromosomes of each original parent. Such a double diploid is termed a polyploid —more specifically, a *tetraploid.*

The tetraploid hybrid would resemble the first-generation hybrid, but the plant as a whole would be larger and somewhat more robust as a consequence of the increased number of chromosomes. More importantly, the tetraploid hybrid would be fully fertile. The meiotic divisions would be normal, since each chromosome now has a regular pairing partner during meiosis (Fig. 10.2). The tetraploid hybrid is a true breeding type; it can perpetuate itself indefinitely. It is, however, reproductively incompatible with its original parental species. If it were to cross with its original parental species, the offspring would be sterile. Hence, the tetraploid hybrid is truly a new distinct species. In but a few generations, we have witnessed essentially the fusion of two old species to form a single derived species.

EXPERIMENTAL VERIFICATION

To return to our wheat story, it may be seen (Fig. 10.1) that the bread wheat contains the chromosome sets of three diploid species—the *AA* of einkorn wheat, the *BB* of *Aegilops speltoides,* and the *CC* of *Aegilops squarrosa.* (The third set is typically referred to by botanists as the *D* genome. It is an accident of nomenclature that the third genome received the letter *D,* rather than *C*). Technically, then, the bread wheat contains six sets of chromosomes. It is said to be a *hexaploid.* The relationships of the three major groups of wheats can be shown as follows:

$$\text{Einkorn} = 14 = \quad AA \quad = \text{diploid}$$
$$\text{Emmer} = 28 = \quad AABB \quad = \text{tetraploid}$$
$$\text{Bread} = 42 = AABBCC = \text{hexaploid}$$

Experimental proof was lacking at the time John Percival proposed that the bread wheats originated from hybridization between the emmer wheat and goat grass, followed by chromosome doubling in the hybrid. Verification awaited an effective method of artificially inducing diploid cells to become polyploid. The search for an efficient chemical inducing agent culminated in the discovery in the late 1930's of colchicine, a substance obtained from the roots of the autumn crocus plant. Treatments of diploid plant cells with colchicine result in a high percentage of polyploid nuclei in the treated plant cells. Colchicine acts on the spindle apparatus of a dividing cell, and prevents a cell from dividing into two daughter halves. The treated undivided cell contains two sets of daughter chromosomes, which ordinarily would have separated from each other had cell division not been impeded. The cell thus comes to possess twice the usual number of chromosomes.

The experimental production of polyploid cells through the application of colchicine paved the way for studies on wheat by E. S. McFadden and E. Sears of the United States Department of Agriculture. These investigators successfully hybridized a tetraploid species of emmer wheat with the diploid wild grass *Aegilops squarrosa*. The chromosome number in the hybrid was doubled by treatment with colchicine. The synthetic hexaploid hybrids were similar in characteristics to natural hexaploid species of bread wheat, and produced functional gametes. At almost the same time, Hitoshi Kihara of Japan obtained a comparable hexaploid wheat species, which spontaneously and naturally had become converted from a sterile hybrid to a fertile hybrid. Kihara's work reinforced the notion that doubling of chromosomes can occur accidentally.

To complete the proof, McFadden and Sears crossed their artificially synthesized hexaploid wheat species with one of the naturally occurring bread wheat *Triticum spelta*. Fully fertile hybrids resulted, removing any doubt that wild grass, a noxious weed, is indeed a parental ancestor of the bread wheats.

COTTON

The story of the cataclysmic evolution of cotton (*Gossypium*) has been partially unraveled by botanical investigators. The evolution of cotton poses some interesting, but unresolved, problems.

Cotton is widely distributed throughout the world, and occurs in both the wild and cultivated state. The cultivated types in the Americas are represented by *Gossypium barbadense*, the prominent cotton of South America, and *Gossypium hirsutum*, grown mainly in Central America and the United States. These two cultivated species of American cotton are of particular interest in that they each possess 52 chromosomes (or 26 pairs) in their cells. Thirteen of these pairs of chromosomes are small and resemble those in wild diploid cotton species still found growing in the Americas; the other 13 pairs are large and like those of diploid cotton species native to the Old World. The Old World cotton ancestor contains the A chromosome set (or genome); the wild American ancestor possesses the D genome. Unquestionably, the present-day American cultivated cotton resulted from a cross between the Old World cotton and the wild American cotton ($AA \times DD$), with subsequent natural duplication of the chromosome complement in the hybrid (AD to $AADD$). The cultivated American cottons are thus tetraploid progenies of two diploid species. The question as to when and where the two diploid progenitors met and hybridized is a thorny one.

Available evidence indicates that the American tetraploid species arose by hybridization in the coastal valleys of Peru in western South America. Many botanists contend that the Old World diploid parent came from southern Asia, having reached South America by dispersal across the Pacific Ocean. The seeds of cotton, however, are not adapted to transportation over great distances by either water or wind. The cotton expert S. C. Harland has suggested that the Old World parent crossed the Pacific by a land bridge in late Cretaceous times, a prehistoric period dating back 135 million years ago. Most modern geologists dismiss as unreasonable the once popular notion of an ancient Pacific land bridge.

Other botanists, particularly J. B. Hutchinson, R. A. Silow, and S. G. Stephens, have argued that the Asiatic diploid cotton was introduced within historic times by civilized man. Early nomadic man from Asia carried the seeds of his crop plants across the Pacific to South America. From hybridizations of the transplanted Old World cotton with wild cotton of the valleys of Peru emerged the superior tetraploid plant. This tetraploid cotton was subsequently introduced into Central America, and then spread to the United States. The South American tetraploids are no longer reproductively compatible with their northern counterparts; hence, the presence today, as remarked earlier, of two distinct species of cultivated cotton in the Americas, *Gossypium barbadense* and *Gossypium hirsutum*.

The reconstruction of the past history of the cultivated American cotton is far from complete. There exists a primitive diploid species of cotton in south Africa, which is regarded as the original forebear of the Old World diploid cottons. The Asiatic cottons were probably derived from the African type. Recently, there has been speculation that the African species of cotton, rather than the Asiatic species, was the immediate parent of the American cotton. This would be in accord with Wegener's theory of Continental Drift. In 1910, the Austrian meteorologist and Arctic explorer Alfred Wegener proposed that the earth's continents had once been a huge

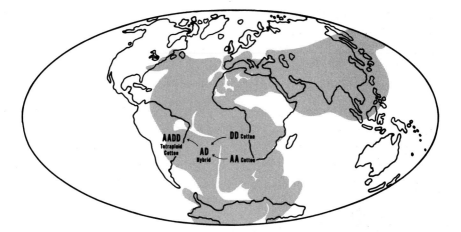

FIG. 10.3. Wegener's Theory of Continental Drift. The present continents were joined in a single land mass ("Pangaea") before the start of the Mesozoic era (about 200 million years ago). Several authors favor the concept of two original large land masses: "Laurasia" in the northern hemisphere and "Gondwanaland" in the southern hemisphere. The hybridization of two African diploid species of cotton to give rise to the American tetraploid species of cotton may have occurred before the continents drifted apart.

land mass (a supercontinent) and have reached their present geographical positions by splitting up and drifting across the ocean floors (Fig. 10.3). The original single land mass, called *Pangaea,* broke up about 150 million years ago. Wegener's theory, earlier ridiculed, has been revived and has gained a measure of scientific respectability in several quarters. Consideration may thus be given to the possibility that an ancestral diploid cotton species of South Africa (genome *A*) at one time overlapped the distribution of another ancestral species (genome *D*) in that part of west Africa which was adjacent to the American continent before continental drift (Fig. 10.3). There hybridization between the two diploid species may have occurred naturally, giving rise to the American tetraploid species which became isolated in northern South America at the time of the parting of the continents. It remains to be seen whether this provocative idea continues to merit attention.

SUGGESTIONS FOR FURTHER READING

BRIGGS, D. and WALTERS, S. M. 1969. *Plant variation and evolution.* New York: McGraw-Hill Book Co.
CURTIS, B. C. and JOHNSTON, D. R. 1969. Hybrid wheat. *Scientific American,* May, pp. 21–29.

HURLEY, P. M. 1968. The confirmation of continental drift. *Scientific American,* April, pp. 53–64.

KURTEN, B. 1969. Continental drift and evolution. *Scientific American,* March, pp. 54–64.

MANGELSDORF, P. C. 1953. Wheat. *Scientific American,* July, pp. 50–59.

STEBBINS, G. L. 1950. *Variation and evolution in plants.* New York: Columbia University Press.

————. 1951. Cataclysmic evolution. *Scientific American,* April, pp. 54–59.

11 Adaptive Radiation

The capacity of a population of organisms to increase its numbers is governed largely by the availability of resources—food, shelter, and space. The available supply of resources in a given environment is limited, whereas the organism's innate ability to multiply is unlimited. A particular environment will soon prove to be inadequate for the number of individuals present. It might thus be expected that some individuals would explore new environments where competition for resources is low. The tendency of individuals to exploit new opportunities is a factor of major significance in the emergence of several new species from an ancestral stock. The successful colonization of previously unoccupied habitats can lead to a rich multitude of diverse species, each better fitted to survive and reproduce under the new conditions than in the ancestral habitat. The spreading of populations into different environments accompanied by divergent adaptive changes of the emigrant populations is referred to as *adaptive radiation.*

GALÁPAGOS ISLANDS

One of the biologically strangest, yet fascinating, areas of the world is an isolated cluster of islands of volcanic origin in the eastern Pacific, the Galápagos Islands. These islands, which Darwin visited for five weeks in 1835, lie on the equator, 600 miles west of Ecuador (Fig. 11.1). The islands are composed wholly of volcanic rock; they were never connected with the mainland of South America. The rugged shoreline cliffs are of gray lava and the coastal lowlands are parched, covered with cacti and thorn brushes. In the humid uplands, tall trees flourish in rich, black soil.

On these islands may be found many distinctive forms of animal life. One of the most unusual is the giant land-dwelling tortoise, which may

111

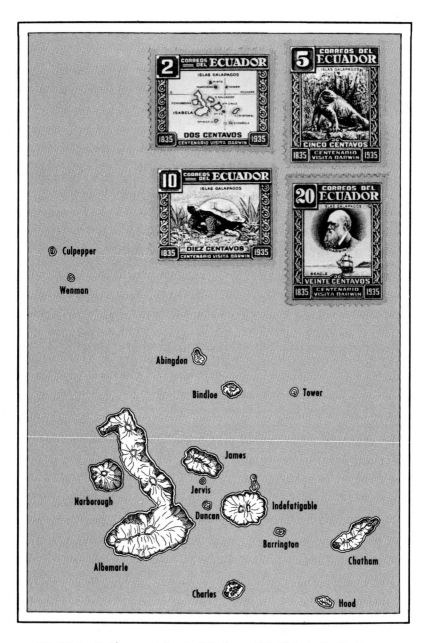

FIG. 11.1. Galápagos Islands ("Enchanted Isles") in the Pacific Ocean, 600 miles west of Ecuador. Darwin had explored this cluster of isolated islands, and found a strange animal life, a "little world within itself." The four stamps shown were issued by Ecuador to commemorate the centenary of Darwin's visit in 1835.

weigh as much as 500 pounds and attain an age of 200 to 250 years. The Spanish word for tortoise, *galápago*, gave the islands their name. Darwin had noticed that the tortoises were clearly different from island to island, although the islands were but a few miles apart. In isolation, each population had evolved its own distinctive features. Yet, all the island tortoises show basic resemblance not only to each other but to relatively large tortoises on the adjacent mainland of South America. The island tortoises doubtless share a common ancestor with the mainland forms. Many years of needless slaying by pirates and whalers pushed the Galápagos tortoises to the brink of extinction. In 1959, a sanctuary was created to protect these remarkable animals.

Still prevalent on the islands are the world's only marine iguana and its inland variety, the land iguana (Fig. 11.2). These two species of prehistoric-looking lizards are ancient arrivals from the mainland. The marine forms occur in colonies on the lava shores, and swim offshore to feed on seaweed. The land iguana lives on leaves and cactus plants. Cactus fills most of the water needs of the land iguana.

FIG. 11.2. Land Iguana on one of the Galápagos Islands. Despite their horrendous appearance, these bizarre inland lizards are mild, torpid, and vegetarians. They feed on leaves and cactus plants. (Courtesy of the American Museum of Natural History.)

At least 85 different kinds of birds have been recorded on the islands. These include rare cormorants which cannot fly, found only on Narborough Island, and flamingos, which breed on James Island. Of particular interest are the small black finches. These black birds exhibit remarkable variations in the structure of the beak and in feeding habits. The finches afford an outstanding example of adaptive radiation. It was the marked diversity within this small group of birds that gave impetus to Darwin's evolutionary views. Darwin had correctly surmised that the diverse finches were modified descendants of the early, rather homogeneous, colonists of the Galápagos. Our present knowledge of these birds, now appropriately called "Darwin's finches," derives largely from the accomplished work of David Lack at Oxford, who visited the Enchanted Isles in 1938.

DARWIN'S FINCHES

Darwin's finches descended from seed-eating birds that inhabited the mainland of South America. The ancestors of Darwin's finches were early migrants to the Galápagos Islands, and probably the first land birds to reach the islands. These early colonists have given rise to 14 distinct species, each well adapted to a specific niche (Fig. 11.3). Thirteen of these species occur in the Galápagos; one is found in the small isolated Cocos Island, northeast of the Galápagos.

The most striking differences between the species are in the sizes and shapes of the beak, which are correlated with marked differences in feeding habits. Six of the species are ground finches, with heavy beaks specialized for crushing seeds. Some of the ground finches live mainly on a diet of seeds found on the ground; others feed primarily on the flowers of prickly pear cacti. The cactus eaters possess decurved, flower-probing beaks. Their beaks are thicker than those of typical flower-eating birds.

All the other species are tree finches, the majority of which feed on insects in the moist forests. One of the most remarkable of these tree dwellers is the woodpecker finch. It possesses a stout, straight beak, but lacks the long tongue characteristic of the true woodpecker. It bores into wood in search of insect larvae like a woodpecker, but then employs a cactus spine or twig to probe out its insect prey from the excavated crevice. Equally extraordinary is the warbler finch, which resembles in form and habit the true warbler. Its slender, warbler-like beak is adapted for picking small insects off bushes. Occasionally, like a warbler, it can capture an insect in flight.

FACTORS IN DIVERSIFICATION

No such great diversity of finches may be found on the South American mainland. In the absence of vacant habitats on the continent, the oc-

FIG. 11.3. Representatives of Darwin's finches. There are 14 species of Darwin's finches, confined to the Galápagos with the exception of one species that inhabits Cocos Island. Closest to the ancestral stock are the six species of ground finches, primarily seed-eaters. The others evolved into eight species of tree finches, the majority of which feed on insects.

casion was lacking for the mainland birds to exploit new situations. However, given the unoccupied habitats on the Galápagos Islands, the opportunity presented itself for the invading birds to evolve in new directions. In the absence of competition, the colonists occupied several ecological habitats, in the dry lowlands as well as the humid uplands. The finches adopted modes of life that ordinarily would not have been opened to them. If true warblers and true woodpeckers had already occupied the islands, it is doubtful that the finches could have evolved into warbler-like and woodpecker-like forms. Thus, *a prime factor promoting adaptive radiation is the absence of competition.*

The emigration of the ancestral finches from the mainland was assuredly not conscious or self-directed. The dispersal of birds from the original home was at random, resulting from the pressure of increasing numbers on the means of subsistence. By chance, some of the birds reached the Galápagos Islands. The original flock of birds that fortuitously arrived at the islands was but a small sample of the parental population, containing at best a limited portion of the parental gene pool. It may be that only a small amount of genetic variation was initially available for selection to work on. What evolutionary changes occurred at the outset were mainly due to random survival (genetic drift). However, the chance element would become less important as the population increased in size. Selection unquestionably became the main evolutionary agent, molding the individual populations into new shapes by the preservation of new favorable mutant or recombination types. More than one island was colonized, and the genetic differentiation of each new local population was promoted by the spatial separation of the islands.

Today we observe that each island is occupied by more than one species of finch. Different species ultimately had spread to various islands. It is axiomatic that two species with identical ecological requirements—utilizing similar resources—cannot coexist indefinitely in the same locality. This is a highly theoretical concept, since it is very unlikely that any two related species can have exactly the same needs. But, if it were at all possible, one species would eventually supplant the other. Accordingly, on islands where several species of finches exist together, we should expect to find that each species is adapted to a different ecological niche. This is precisely what we encounter. The three common species of ground finches—small (*Geospiza fuliginosa*), medium (*Geospiza fortis*), and large (*Geospiza magnirostris*)—occur together in the coastal lowlands of several islands. Each species, however, is specialized in feeding on a seed of a certain size. The small-beaked *Geospiza fuliginosa*, for example, feeds on small grass seeds, whereas the large-beaked *Geospiza magnirostris* eats large hard fruits. Different species, with different food requirements, can thus exist together in an environment with varied food resources.

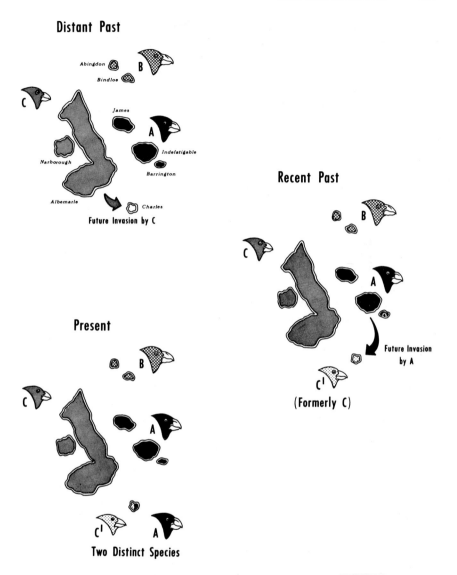

FIG. 11.4. Historical events leading to the existence today of two distinct species of tree finches, *Camarhynchus psittacula* (designated A) and *Camarhynchus pauper* (C'), which occur together on Charles Island. Charles Island had been colonized by finches on two separate occasions. The earlier immigrant came from Albemarle Island in the distant past; the later immigrant was a more recent arrival from Indefatigable or Barrington. The two immigrating groups, although initially only races of the same species, had accumulated sufficient genetic differences in isolation that they did not interbreed when they met on Charles Island. Thus, they are separate species. (Based on the extensive studies by David Lack.)

GEOGRAPHIC SPECIATION

In an earlier chapter the view was presented that geographic or spatial isolation is an important, if not essential, condition for the formation of a new species. When two populations are separated by a geographical barrier, each may diverge independently of the other. The distribution of insectivorous tree finches on some of the Galápagos Islands attests to the significance of geographical isolation in the speciation process.

One particular assemblage of tree finches has a widespread distribution (Fig. 11.4). These finches presently exhibit a discrete, or discontinuous, pattern of geographical variation. If we were able to gaze into the evolutionary past, we would probably witness the series of events depicted in Figure 11.4. At one time, we would be able to recognize three well-defined geographical groups, which, for simplicity of presentation, may be designated A, B, and C. We might then subsequently observe the Albemarle form (C) spreading to Charles Island and establishing a colony, which, in time, differentiated into group C'. The Albemarle finch today does show a close resemblance to the Charles form, which suggests that the latter was derived from the former. If we were to stop the evolutionary clock at this time, we would properly regard this assemblage of finches as a single species, subdivided into four well-marked geographic races. In fact, this assemblage has been designated as one species, *Camarhynchus psittacula*.

At the present time, we find that Charles Island is inhabited not only by group C' but also by a newly established colony, whose members are indistinguishable from those of group A. Undoubtedly, the A group on Charles Island comprises recent arrivals from one of the central islands, Indefatigable or Barrington.

The more recent immigrants, group A, on Charles occur together with the older colonists, group C', but they do *not* interbreed. Thus, the two groups, having arisen initially from separate islands, had developed sufficient genetic differences in isolation to remain distinct when they met on Charles Island. Groups A and C' are two separate species, actually designated as *Camarhynchus psittacula* and *Camarhynchus pauper*, respectively.

This situation raises some interesting questions. If group C on Albemarle were now to spread to Abingdon, where B occurs, and exchange of genes did not take place between them, then B and C would be considered as distinct species. But, as far as we know, C has not invaded the territory of B, and the proper designation of the two groups cannot be made. Most evolutionists would probably regard B and C as races, or subspecies, of the same species, *Camarhynchus psittacula*. Regardless of the correct terminology, the important consideration is the demonstration that species formation is preceded by geographical separation.

CLASSIFICATION

The original ancestral stock of finches on the Galápagos diverged along several different paths. The pattern of divergence is reflected in the biologists' scheme of classification of organisms. All the finches are related to one another, but the various species of ground finches obviously are more related by descent to one another than to the members of the tree-finch assemblage. As a measure of evolutionary affinities, the ground finches are grouped together in one genus (*Geospiza*) and the tree finches are clustered in another genus (*Camarhynchus*). The different lineages of finches are portrayed in Figure 11.5. It should be clear that our classification scheme is simply nothing more than an expression of evolutionary relationships between groups of organisms.

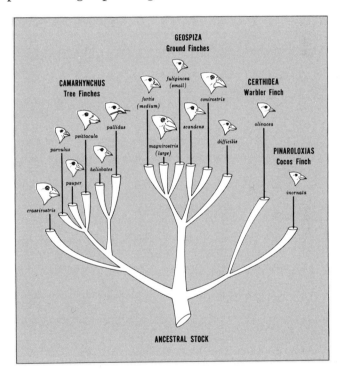

FIG. 11.5. Evolutionary tree of Darwin's finches, graphically expressing what is known or surmised as to the degree of relationship or kinship between the different species of finches. Darwin's finches evolved from a common stock, and are represented today by 14 species. The species are assembled in four genera, of which two (Certhidea and Pinaroloxias) contain only a single species each. The species associated together in a genus have significant common attributes, judged to denote evolutionary affinities. (Based on the findings of David Lack.)

In the next chapter we shall see how adaptive radiation on a much larger scale than that which occurred in the finches led to the origin of radically new assemblages of organisms, distinguishable as orders and classes by the taxonomist.

SUGGESTIONS FOR FURTHER READING

LACK, D. 1947. *Darwin's finches.* London: Cambridge University Press.
————. 1953. Darwin's finches. *Scientific American*, April, pp. 66–72.
SMITH, J. M. 1958. *The theory of evolution.* Baltimore: Penguin Books, Inc.

12 Major Adaptive Radiations

The diversity of Darwin's finches is the outcome of successful invasion by migrants from the mainland of the variety of vacant habitats on the Galápagos Islands. The pattern of adaptive radiation manifested by Darwin's finches has been imitated repeatedly by different forms of life. Organisms throughout the ages have seized new opportunities open to them by the absence of competitors and have diverged in the new environments. The habitats available to Darwin's finches were certainly few in number in comparison to the enormous range of ecological habitats in the world. The larger the region and the more diverse the environmental conditions, the greater the variety of life.

Approximately 400 million years ago, during a period of history referred to by geologists as the Devonian, the vast areas of land were monotonously barren of animal life. Save for rare creatures like scorpions and millipedes, animal life of those distant years was confined to the water. The seas were crowded with invertebrate animals of varied kinds. The fresh and salt waters contained a highly diversified and abundant assemblage of cartilaginous and bony fishes. The vacant terrestrial regions were not to remain long unoccupied. From one of the many groups of fishes inhabiting the pools and swamps in the Devonian period emerged the first land vertebrate. The initial modest step onto land started the vertebrates on their conquest of all available terrestrial habitats. This chapter tells the story of the origin and diversification of the backboned land dwellers.

INVASION OF LAND

Prominent among the numerous Devonian aquatic forms were the lobe-finned fishes, the Crossopterygii, which possessed the ability to gulp air when they rose to the surface. These ancient air-breathing fishes repre-

121

sent the stock from which the first land vertebrates, the amphibians, were derived (Fig. 12.1). The factors that led these ancestral lobe-finned fishes to venture onto land are unknown. The impelling force might have been population pressure or simply the inherent tendency of individuals, particularly of the young, to disperse. A. S. Romer of Harvard University has advanced the irresistible conjecture that the crossopterygians were forced to crawl on dry land on those occasions when the pools they inhabited became fowl, stagnant, or completely dry. There is convincing geological

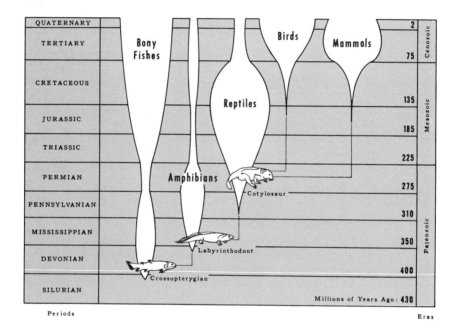

FIG. 12.1. Evolution of land vertebrates in the geologic past.
From air-breathing, lobe-finned fishes (crossopterygians) emerged the first four-footed land inhabitants, the amphibians. Primitive amphibians (labyrinthodonts) gave rise to the reptiles, the first vertebrates to become firmly established on land. The birds and mammals owe their origin to an early reptilian stock (cotylosaurs). An important biological principle reveals itself: each new vertebrate group did not arise from highly developed or advanced members of the ancestral group, but rather from early primitive forms near the base of the ancestral stock. The thickness of the various branches provides a rough measure of the comparative abundance of the five vertebrate groups during geologic history. The Devonian period is often called the "Age of Fishes"; the Mississippian and Pennsylvanian periods (frequently lumped together as the Carboniferous period) are referred to as the "Age of Amphibians"; the Mesozoic era is the grand "Age of Reptiles"; and the Cenozoic era is the "Age of Mammals."

evidence that the Devonian years were marked by excessive seasonal droughts. It is not unimaginable that the water in some pools periodically evaporated. The suggestion, then, is that the crossopterygians wriggled out of stagnant and shrinking water holes onto land to seek pools elsewhere in which water still remained. Thus, paradoxically, the first actual movements on land might not have been at all associated with an attempt to abandon aquatic existence, but rather to retain it.

The above hypothesis is admittedly speculative. However, the fact remains that those crossopterygians that emerged on land, though crudely adapted for terrestrial existence, did not encounter any competitors that could immediately spell doom to their awkward initial trial on land. It is also instructive to note that the lobe-finned fishes did possess certain capacities that would prove to be important under the new conditions of life. Evolutionists speak of such potential adaptive characters as *preadaptations*.

The preadaptations of the lobe-finned fishes included primitive membranous lungs and internal nostrils, both of which are important for atmospheric breathing. It should be understood that such preadapted characters were not favorably selected with a view to their possible utility in some future mode of life. There is no foresight or design in the selection process. Nor do mutational changes occur in anticipation of some new environmental condition. A trait is selected only when it imparts an advantage to the organism in its immediate environment. Accordingly, lungs in the crossopterygians did not evolve with conscious reference toward a possible future land life, but only because such a structure was important, if not essential, to the survival of these air-breathing fishes.

The crossopterygians did not, of course, possess typical amphibian limbs. However, their lateral fins contained fleshy lobes, within which were bony elements basically comparable to those of a limb of a terrestrial vertebrate. Figure 12.2 shows a restoration of a widespread Devonian form, *Eusthenopteron*, in which the lateral fins had developed into stout muscular paddles.

Before the close of the Devonian period, the transition from fish to amphibian had been completed. The early land-living amphibians were slim-bodied with fishlike tails, but they possessed limbs capable of locomotion on land. The four-footed amphibian flourished in the humid coal swamps of Mississippian and Pennsylvanian times, but they never did become completely adapted for existence on land. All the ancient amphibians, such as *Diplovertebron* (Fig. 12.2), spent much of their lives in water, and their modern descendants, the salamanders, newts, frogs, and toads, must return to water to deposit their eggs. Thus, the amphibians were the first vertebrates to colonize land, but they were, and still are, only partially adapted for terrestrial life.

FIG. 12.2. Stages in the transition of the lobe-finned fishes into amphibians, as reconstructed by W. K. Gregory and painted by Francis Lee Jaques. *Bottom,* the primitive Devonian air-breathing crossopterygian, *Eusthenopteron,* floundering on a stream bank with its muscular, paddle-like fins. *Top,* the Pennsylvanian tailed amphibian, *Diplovertebron,* with limbs capable of true locomotion on land. Much of the life of this early tetrapod was spent in water. (Courtesy of the American Museum of Natural History.)

CONQUEST OF LAND

From the amphibians emerged the reptiles, true terrestrial forms. The appearance of a shell-covered egg, which can be laid on land, freed the reptile from dependence upon water. The elimination of a water-dwelling stage was a major evolutionary advance. The terrestrial egg-laying habit evolved very early in reptilian evolution, and probably first arose in a reptile-like form that lived an amphibian existence. The earliest and most primitive reptiles, known as the cotylosaurs, made their appearance in the Pennsylvanian period, about 300 million years ago. *Seymouria*, shown in Figure 12.3, is a representative of this group from the early Permian

FIG. 12.3. Seymouria, a transitional form from Permian times (275 million years ago) that bridges the gap between amphibians and reptiles. It is not known whether the eggs (depicted here in moist sand) were laid on land or in the water. *Seymouria* is generally regarded as a member of a primitive group of reptiles, the cotylosaurs, the basal stock from which all other reptiles arose. (From a painting by Francis Lee Jaques; courtesy of the American Museum of Natural History.)

rocks of Texas. This fossil form exhibits such a mixture of amphibian and reptilian skeletal features that authorities disagree as to its correct classification. This difficulty in properly assigning *Seymouria* should not be at all disconcerting. Rather, it calls attention to the gradual transition from amphibians to reptiles, and vividly reinforces the validity of our concept of evolution.

The earliest reptile probably deposited its eggs in water, much like an amphibian. We may surmise that many eggs, especially those deposited in shallow pools subject to evaporation, failed to develop. Any mutational changes that would promote the chances of survival of the embryos would be selectively advantageous. Perhaps, then, the first step in the evolution of the shelled egg was the selective advantage of eggs capable of developing ashore rather than in the water itself. It would thus appear that the earliest reptiles were not, as often popularly imagined, first fully terrestrial in adult life and then only later did a land egg emerge. Rather, the terrestrial egg had its beginnings in reptile-like forms that were essentially aquatic. Then, with the perfection of the shelled egg, the reptiles moved inland and exploited the wide expanses of land areas. The ancestral reptilian stock initiated one of the most spectacular adaptive radiations in life's history. The reptiles were the dominant land animals of the earth for a duration well over one hundred million years. The Mesozoic era, during which the reptiles thrived, is often referred to as the Age of Reptiles.

Figure 12.4 reveals the variety of reptiles that blossomed from the basal stock, the cotylosaurs. By far the most awe-inspiring and famous were the dinosaurs, which reigned over the lands until the close of the Mesozoic era before suffering extinction. The dinosaurs were remarkably diverse; they varied in size, bodily form, and habits. Some of the dinosaurs were carnivorous, such as the brutish *Tyrannosaurus*, whereas others were vegetarians, such as the feeble-toothed but ponderous *Brontosaurus*. Not all dinosaurs were immense; some were no bigger than chickens. The dinosaurs were descended from the thecodonts—slender, fast-running, lizard-like creatures. In fact, there were two great groups of dinosaurs, the Saurischia and the Ornithischia (Fig. 12.4), which evolved independently from two different lines of the thecodonts.

The thecodonts gave rise as well to bizarre reptiles that took to the air, the pterosaurs. These "dragons of the air" possessed highly expansive wings and disproportionately short bodies. It would seem that the huge membranous wings developed at the sacrificial expanse of the body. The winged pterosaurs succumbed before the end of the Mesozoic era. Another independent branch of the thecodonts led to eminently more successful flyers, the birds. The origin of birds from reptiles is revealed by the celebrated *Archaeopteryx*, a Jurassic form (Fig. 12.4) that was essentially

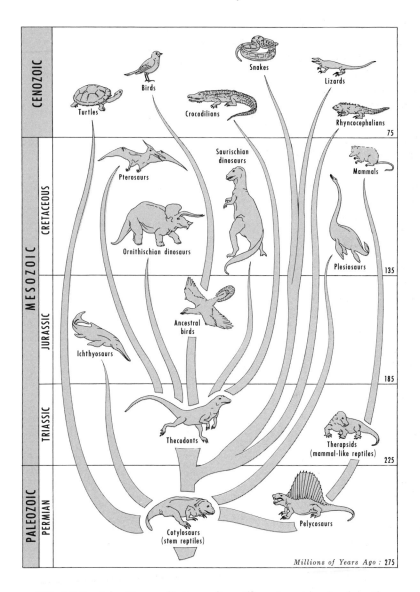

FIG. 12.4. Adaptive radiation of reptiles. A vast horde of reptiles came into existence from the basal stock, the cotylosaurs, at the beginning of the Mesozoic era, roughly 225 million years ago. This matchless assemblage of reptiles was triumphant for a duration well over 100 million years. Then, before the close of the Mesozoic era, the great majority of reptiles passed into oblivion. (Redrawn, with modification, from E. H. Colbert, *The Dinosaur Book*, McGraw-Hill Book Company, copyright 1951, by the American Museum of Natural History.)

an air-borne lizard. This feathered creature possessed a slender, lizard-like tail and a scaly head equipped with reptilian teeth.

Certain reptiles returned to water. The streamlined, dolphin-like ichthyosaurs and the long-necked, short-bodied plesiosaurs were marine, fish-eating reptiles. These aquatic reptiles breathed by means of lungs; they certainly did not redevelop the gills of their very distant fish ancestors. Indeed, it is axiomatic that a structure once lost in the long course of evolution cannot be regained. This is the doctrine of irreversibility of evolution, or *Dollo's law*, after Louis Dollo, the eminent Belgian paleontologist to whom the principle is ascribed.

Among the early reptiles present at the beginning of Mesozoic days were the pelycosaurs, notable for their peculiar sail-like extensions of the back (Fig. 12.5). The function of the gaudy "sail" is unknown, but it

FIG. 12.5. Dimetrodon, one of the pelycosaurs that flourished during Permian times. The gaudy "sail" may have served as a heat-regulating device. (From a restoration by Charles R. Knight; courtesy of the American Museum of Natural History.)

should not be thought that this structural feature was merely ornamental or useless. As emphatically stated in earlier chapters, traits of organisms are selected with reference to their adaptive utility. Means of maintaining a stable body temperature are poorly developed in reptiles. It is not inconceivable that the pelycosauran "sail" was a functional device to achieve some degree of heat regulation. Be that as it may, the pelycosaurs gave rise to an important group of reptiles, the therapsids. These mammal-like forms bridged the structural gap between the reptiles and the mammals (Fig. 12.4).

EXTINCTION AND REPLACEMENT

The history of the reptiles attests to the ultimate fate of many groups of organisms—*extinction*. The reptilian dynasty collapsed before the close of the Mesozoic era. Of the vast host of Mesozoic reptiles, relatively few have survived to modern times, among them the lizards, snakes, crocodiles, and turtles. The famed land dinosaurs, the great marine plesiosaurs and ichthyosaurs, and the flying pterosaurs all became extinct. The cause of the decline and death of the tremendous array of reptiles is obscure. Some authors have attributed the demise of the giant reptiles to some radical change in environmental conditions to which the reptiles could not adapt. Other writers have variously placed the blame on disease, parasites, over-specialization, excessive oxygen from plants, the wholesale devouring of the reptilian eggs by small mammals, and the development of psychotic suicidal tendencies. The most judicious scientific explanation is simply— "No one knows."

In 1966, the internationally known oceanographer Bruce C. Heezen, of the Lamont Geological Observatory, Columbia University, related the mass extinctions of organisms throughout history to periodic reversals of the magnetic field above the earth's atmosphere. Extending far out into space, the magnetic field normally shields the earth from most of the potentially lethal cosmic radiation. When, however, the magnetic field weakens and collapses, the full force of cosmic radiation strikes the surface of the earth. Every 50 million years the magnetic field apparently decreases in strength, allowing at least 500 roentgens of radiation to bombard the earth. This intense radiation might explain the disappearance of the giant reptiles. Heezen predicts that the magnetic field will weaken again by A.D. 4000. Then, according to his theory, a new biological upheaval or catastrophe will befall the earth.

Whatever may be the cause of mass extinctions, the fact remains that as one group of organisms recedes and dies out completely, another group spreads and evolves. The decline of the reptiles provided evolutionary opportunities for the birds and the mammals. The vacancies in the habitats were now to be occupied by these warm-blooded vertebrates. Small and inconspicuous during the Mesozoic era, the mammals ascended to unquestionable dominancy during the Cenozoic era, which began approximately 75 million years ago. The mammals diversified into marine forms (*e.g.*, the whale, dolphin, seal, and walrus), fossorial forms living underground (*e.g.*, the mole), flying and gliding animals (*e.g.*, the bat and flying squirrel), and cursorial types well-adapted for running (*e.g.*, the horse).

The various mammalian groups are, of course, adapted to their different modes of life. The appendages, for example, are specialized for flight, swimming, or movement on land. An important lesson may be drawn from the variety of specialized appendages. Superficially there is scant resemblance between the arm of a man, the flipper of a whale, and the wing of a bat. And yet, a close comparison of the skeletal elements (Fig. 12.6) shows that the structural design, bone for bone, is basically the same. The differences are mainly in the relative lengths of the component bones. In the forelimb of the bat, for instance, the metacarpals and phalanges (except those of the thumb) are greatly elongated. Although highly modified, the bones of the bat's wing are not fundamentally different from those of other mammals. The conclusion is inescapable that the limb bones of man, the bat, and the whale are modifications of a common ancestral pattern. The facts admit of no other logical interpretation. Indeed, as seen in Figure 12.5, the forelimbs of all tetrapod vertebrates exhibit a unity of anatomical pattern intelligible only on the basis of common inheritance. The corresponding limb bones of tetrapod vertebrates are said to be *homologous*, since they are structurally identical with those in the common ancestor. In contrast, the wing of a bird and the wing of a butterfly are *analogous;* both are used for flight, but they are built on an entirely different structural plan.

EVOLUTION OF HORSES

The cardinal feature of adaptive radiation is the emergence from a central, generalized stock of a large number of divergent branches or lineages. Not all branches persist; indeed, the general rule is that all but a few perish. The disappearance of many branches in the distant past may lead the observer today to the mistaken impression that the evolution of a particular group was not at all intricately forked. Thus, the evolution of horses is commonly, but erroneously, depicted as an undeviating, straight-line progression from the small, terrier-sized *Hyracotherium* (better known as *Eohippus*, the "dawn horse") to the large modern horse, *Equus*. On the contrary, the detailed work of modern paleontologists, prominent among

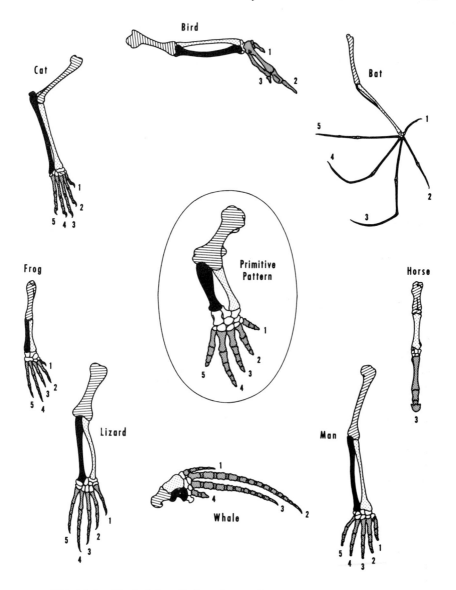

FIG. 12.6. Varied forelimbs of vertebrates, all of which are built on the same structural plan. The best explanation for the fundamentally similar framework of bones is that man and all other vertebrates share a common ancestry. Homologous bones are indicated as follows: humerus (upper arm)—crosshatching; radius (forearm)—light stippling; ulna (forearm)—black; carpals (wrist)—white; metacarpals (palm) and phalanges (digits)—heavy stippling. The number of phalanges in each digit is indicated by a numeral, beginning with the first digit (thumb).

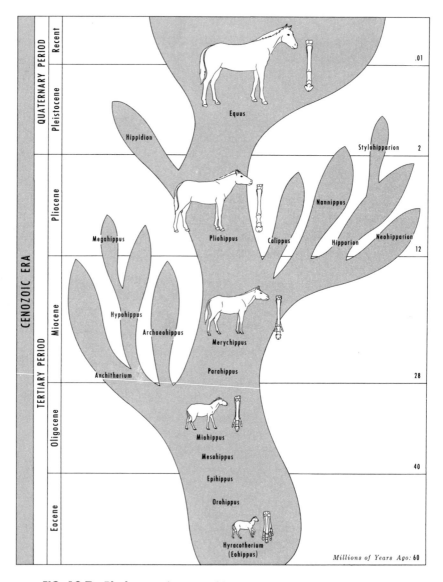

FIG. 12.7. Phylogenetic tree of horses through time, with its many divergent branches. All branches died out, save one which eventually culminated in the modern group of horses, *Equus*. The history of horses dates back to early Cenozoic times, some 60 million years ago. (The Cenozoic era is divided into *periods*, which in turn are subdivided into *epochs*.)

them being G. G. Simpson, has revealed convincingly a pattern of many divergent lineages. The major lineages directly or indirectly involved in the ascension of the modern horse are shown in Figure 12.7.

The ancestry of horses can be traced back to the beginning of the Eocene epoch, some 60 million years ago. The diminutive *Hyracotherium* was about 10 inches high and had four functional toes on the front foot and three on the hind. It was not adapted for speed and browsed on the soft leaves and fruits of bushes. This dawn horse could scarcely have grazed on harsh grass, as its molar teeth had low crowns and very weak grinding surfaces. *Hyracotherium* spread over North America and Europe, but the European assemblage left no descendants. The derivatives of the North American dawn horse in the Eocene were *Orohippus* and *Epihippus*, and these gradually gave way to more progressive kinds of horses in the Oligocene, *Mesohippus* and *Miohippus*. Both of these Oligocene horses were about 24 inches high with only three toes on each foot, but they remained browsers with low-crowned teeth. The *Miohippus* stock subsequently branched radially into a variety of types that lived in the Miocene epoch. Most of the Miocene offshoots (*e.g.*, *Anchitherium* and *Hypohippus*) continued the browsing habits of their ancestors. However, one stock —*Merychippus*—had successfully exploited a new mode of life associated with the expansion of grasslands in Miocene times. *Merychippus* was the first true grazing form, well equipped with high-crowned, complexly ridged teeth effective in grinding stout grass.

From the slow-footed, three-toed *Merychippus* emerged the fleet-footed, one-toed *Pliohippus* during the Pliocene epoch. The appearance of the one-toed condition was a landmark in horse history, an event doubtlessly fostered by natural selection. Grazing horses in the open, grassy plains were subject to appreciable predation from carnivores. Natural selection favored reduction of the toes, lightening the legs for speed. However, not all descendants of *Merychippus* evolved the progressive single-toed condition. Several lines of Pliocene horses, such as *Hipparion* and *Nannippus*, retained the conservative three-toed pattern. These conservative Pliocene horses represent evolutionary blind alleys, removed from the main line of ancestry of the modern horse (Fig. 12.7). Only *Pliohippus*, the first one-toed horse, remained to become the progenitor of the modern form, *Equus*. The modern horse arose in North America at the close of the Pliocene epoch, and spread rapidly over most of the world. Ironically, *Equus* inexplicably vanished in North America a few thousand years ago, before the arrival of the first white colonist. The modern horse was reintroduced from Europe in the early 1500's by the Spaniards. All present-day horses are domestic; it is doubtful if there are any existing stocks of truly wild horses that are not descendants of populations at one time domesticated.

13 Convergence

We have learned that a population of organisms tends to become highly diversified when it spreads over an area with varied habitats. The population can diverge into radically different lines, each modified for a specific ecological role. Now, essentially similar habitats may be found in widely separate parts of the world. It would therefore not be surprising to find that two groups of organisms, unrelated by descent but living under similar environmental conditions in different geographic regions, can exhibit similarities in habits and general appearances. The tendency of one group of organisms to develop superficial resemblances to another group of different ancestry is called *convergence*.

Convergence is not an uncommon phenomenon in nature. Many unrelated, or remotely related, organisms have converged in appearance as a consequence of exploitation of habitats of similar ecological makeup. The relationship of convergence to adaptive radiation should be evident; the former is the inevitable result of the countless series of adaptive radiations that have taken place in scattered parts of the globe. Striking examples of convergence are afforded by the living marsupials of Australia and the archaic hoofed mammals of South America.

MARSUPIALS OF AUSTRALIA

The massive island continent of Australia has long been isolated from Asia, at least since the commencement of the Cenozoic era, the last 75 million years. It is on this isolated island that the marsupials, primitive pouched mammals, survived, free from the competition of the more efficient placental mammals when they came into prominence. In the absence of a land migration route between Asia and Australia, the latter land mass was inaccessible to practically all the placental mammals. On other continents, the marsupials perished, save for the peculiar American opossums, the didelphids.

Imprisoned in Australia, the marsupials spread into a variety of habitats. Several live in the open plains and grasslands; some are tree-dwellers; others are burrowers; and still others are gliders (Fig. 13.1). Most kangaroos are terrestrial, but one variety, the monkeylike kangaroo, is arboreal. The slow-moving, nocturnal "teddy bear," koala, lives and feeds on Eucalyptus, the dominant tree of Australia. The bandicoot, with rabbitlike ears, has sturdy claws adapted for digging in the ground in search of insects. Marsupial moles live in desert burrows, and flying phalangers have

Banded Anteater

Wombat

Marsupial Mouse

Koala

Flying Phalanger

Rabbit Bandicoot

Tasmanian Wolf

FIG. 13.1. Marsupials, or pouched mammals, of Australia, illustrating the twin themes of adaptive radiation and convergence. The marsupials have radiated, or diversified, into a variety of forms, ranging from the tiny insect-eating jumping "mouse" to the fierce, flesh-eating Tasmanian "wolf." Many of the marsupials resemble in appearance and habit the placental mammals of other parts of the world, although they are *not* closely related to them.

webs of loose skin stretched between the forelimbs and hindlimbs. The flying phalanger cannot actually fly, but is adept at gliding. The impressive diversity of marsupials thus represents an admirable example of adaptive radiation.

The marsupials of Australia also vividly illustrate the phenomenon of convergence. They have filled the ecological niches normally occupied by placental mammals in other parts of the world. The marsupials "mouse," "mole," "anteater," "wolf," flying phalanger, and groundhog-like wombat strikingly resemble the true placental types—mouse, mole, anteater, wolf, flying squirrel, and groundhog, respectively—in general appearance and in ways of life.

It is of interest to note that a marsupial "bat" has not evolved in Australia. The opportunity was apparently denied by the invasion of placental bats from Asia, one of the few placental forms that managed, probably as a result of dispersal by flight and winds, to reach Australia. With the coming of man, the secure existence of the marsupials has been threatened. Prehistoric man introduced dogs, which ran wild (the dingos), and later settlers brought a number of European placental mammals, such as the rabbit, hare, fox, and Norway rat. Among the marsupials faced with extinction are the marsupial "wolf," which survives today only in Tasmania and the slow-moving banded "anteater," which is rapidly disappearing.

ANCIENT HOOFED MAMMALS OF SOUTH AMERICA

When the great majority of land mammals first arose, South America was just as much an island continent as Australia. An astonishingly rich assemblage of mammals evolved in isolation in South America during the 70 million years or more that the continent remained separated from the rest of the world. Such bizarre placental mammals emerged as the giant ground sloth, the enormous toothless anteater, and the armored armadillo-like glyptodont.

The crowd of mammals that arose is so bewildering that we had best confine our attention to one group—the herbivorous hoofed mammals (ungulates). Even here it is difficult to call up a true picture of the tremendous variety of ungulate types. These archaic hoofed mammals are quite unfamiliar to most people; they have no vernacular names and indeed taxonomists have had to create special suborders for many of them. Selected examples are shown in Figure 13.2. Prominent among the hoofed mammals was the massive *Toxodon*, whose appearance may be likened to a hornless rhinoceros or a hippopotamus. Skeletal remains of this ponderous creature were first found by Charles Darwin when he disembarked from the H. M. S. *Beagle* to explore the vast, treeless pampas of Argentina.

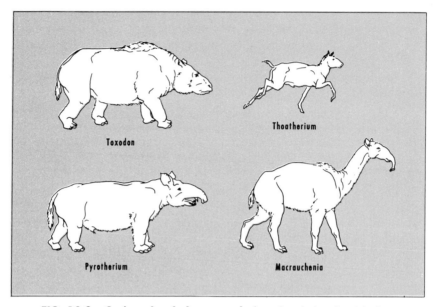

FIG. 13.2. Curious hoofed mammals (ungulates) that flourished on the continent of South America some 60 to 70 million years ago, and have long since vanished from the scene. These fascinating ungulates illustrate the principle of convergence. *Toxodon* superficially resembles a rhinoceros, *Thoatherium* has the appearance of a horse, *Pyrotherium* may be likened to an elephant, and *Macrauchenia* looks like a camel.

Another fossil remain that attracted Darwin's attention was the skeleton of *Macrauchenia*, which he erroneously thought was clearly related to the camel because of the structure of the bones of its long neck. Other remarkable creatures were the huge *Pyrotherium*, resembling an elephant, and the light and graceful single-toed *Thoatherium*, rivaling the horse. These South American forms bear only superficial resemblances to the hoofed mammals in other parts of the world. The similarities in external appearances signify convergence, and not relationship by descent.

These outlandish South American hoofed mammals, evolving independently of mammalian types in North America, thrived for many millions of years. Then the water gap between the Americas was closed. The Isthmus of Panama rose above the sea, establishing a land corridor linking the two continents. Through this land bridge infiltrated a horde of northern invaders. Predatory carnivores, such as saber-toothed tigers and wolves, entered South America from the north, as did progressive herbivorous ungulates, among which were tapirs, peccaries, llamas, and deers. All of the native South American hoofed mammals, without exception, were driven into extinction.

PARALLELISM

Convergence, as we have just seen, is the development of superficial resemblances between organisms of quite different ancestral stocks. Under similar environmental conditions, two unrelated organisms may come to resemble one another. Evolutionists have come to discern another important pattern in nature, akin to convergence yet distinguishable. This is the phenomenon of parallelism, whereby two organisms acquire similar characteristics independently of one another, but have stemmed from related ancestral stocks. The concept of parallelism has been invoked to illuminate some of the puzzling problems of biogeography, the geographic distribution of organisms.

One challenging problem concerns the degree of relationship of New World and Old World porcupines, the familiar spine-bearing rodents. The New World porcupines are native to South America; their counterparts in North America are relatively recent immigrants from the South American forests. The Old World porcupines are common in Africa and have spread into southern parts of Eurasia. Some students of the subject believe that the South American porcupines are direct descendants of the African forms. It has been suggested that the African porcupines crossed the South Atlantic on raftlike floating objects. A transoceanic dispersal route, however, seems improbable to several authorities. An alternative explanation, championed by the paleontologist Albert Wood of Amherst College, is that the South American and African porcupines have been derived independently of each other from an ancient generalized (non-porcupine) rodent stock which inhabited both the New World and Old World. Thus, the South American and African porcupines share a common ancestor (a primitive rodent stock), but independently, in parallel fashion, acquired structural resemblances. This interpretation is weakened by our imperfect knowledge of the basal stock from which arose the two separate lineages of porcupines. Nonetheless, the thesis of parallel evolution is quite plausible.

SUGGESTIONS FOR FURTHER READING

BARNETT, L. and the Editors of *Life*. 1960. *The wonders of life on earth*. New York: Time, Inc. Book Division.
HOTTON, N. 1968. *The evidence of evolution*. New York: American Heritage Publishing Co., Inc.
SIMPSON, G. G. 1964. *This view of life*. New York: Harcourt, Brace & World, Inc.

14 Origin and History of Life

We have been unceasingly taught not to believe in spontaneous generation, the view that living things can originate from lifeless matter. The classical experiments of Francesco Redi, Lazzaro Spallanzani, and Louis Pasteur provided proof that new life can only come from existing life. However, these experiments revealed only that life cannot arise spontaneously under conditions that exist on earth today. Conditions on the primeval earth billions of years ago were assuredly different from those of the present, and the first form of life, or self-duplicating particle, did arise spontaneously from chemical inanimate substances.

PRIMITIVE EARTH

The view that life emerged by a long and gradual process of chemical evolution was first convincingly set forth by the Russian biochemist, A. I. Oparin, in 1924, in an enthralling book entitled *The Origin of Life.* The transformation of lifeless chemicals into living matter extended over some two billion years. Such a transformation, as Oparin points out, is no longer possible today. If by pure chance a living particle approaching that of the first form of life should now appear, it would be rapidly decomposed by the oxygen of the air or be quickly destroyed by the countless microorganisms presently populating the earth.

Our earth is estimated to be 4 billion to 5 billion years old. It originated by the gradual concentration of whirling clouds of dust and gas into a large sphere. The primitive earth was initially a molten mass with such intense heat as to not permit even the existence of water in the liquid state. As the earth slowly cooled, the outer surface of the molten ball hardened into a thin layer or crust of crystalline rock. Jagged land masses were gradually built up as molten rock poured out through volcano-like crevices in the earth's surface. Water vapor and other volcanic gases enveloped the surface to form the primitive atmosphere. The seas came into existence when the atmospheric water vapor condensed into drops and fell as rain.

The atmosphere of the primitive earth was quite unlike our present atmosphere. Common components like free oxygen (O_2) and carbon dioxide (CO_2) were virtually absent. Oxygen was bound in the form of water and metallic oxides; carbon was not linked with oxygen but rather was combined with hydrogen and metals of the earth's crust. Accordingly, it is important to note that any complex organic compound that should arise during this early time would not be subject to decomposition by free oxygen.

The earth's early atmosphere was rich in hydrogen; today, the earth has scarcely any free hydrogen. The hydrogen (H_2) of the primitive earth chemically united with carbon to form methane (CH_4), with nitrogen to form ammonia (NH_3), and with oxygen to form water vapor (H_2O). The water vapor that fell as rain eroded the rocks and washed minerals into the seas. The stage was set for the combination of chemical elements. Chemicals from the atmosphere mixed and reacted with those in the waters to form a wealth of hydrocarbons, which are compounds of hydrogen and carbon. Water, hydrocarbons, and ammonia comprise the raw materials of amino acids, which, in turn, are the building blocks for large molecules (proteins). Thus, in the primitive sea, amino acids accumulated in considerable quantities and were joined together to form proteins.

Complex carbon compounds such as amino acids and proteins are termed "organic" because they are made by living organisms. Our present-day green plants use the energy of sunlight to synthesize organic compounds from simple molecules. What, then, was the energy source in the primitive earth, and how was synthesis of organic compounds effected in the absence of living things? It is generally held that ultraviolet rays from the sun, electrical discharges such as lightning, and dry heat from volcanic activity furnished the means to join the simple carbon compounds and nitrogenous substances into amino acids. Is there a valid basis for such a widely accepted view?

EXPERIMENTAL SYNTHESIS OF ORGANIC COMPOUNDS

In the early days of chemistry, it was believed that organic compounds could be produced only by living organisms. But, in 1828, Friedrich Wöhler succeeded in manufacturing the organic compound *urea* under artificial conditions in the laboratory. Since Wöhler's discovery, a large variety of organic chemicals (amino acids, monsaccharides, purines, and vitamins) formerly produced only in organisms have been artificially synthesized.

Approximately two decades ago, in 1953, Stanley Miller, then at the University of Chicago and a student of Nobel laureate Harold Urey, synthesized organic compounds under conditions simulating the primitive atmosphere of the earth. He passed electrical sparks through a mixture of hydrogen, water, ammonia, and methane. The electrical discharges duplicated the effects of violent electrical storms in the primitive universe. The four simple inorganic molecules interacted, after a mere week, to form several kinds of amino acids, among them being alanine, glycine, aspartic acid, and glutamic acid.

High energy radiations, such as cosmic rays, are also instrumental in producing organic compounds. Melvin Calvin of the University of California at Berkeley irradiated solutions of carbon dioxide and water in a cyclotron and obtained formic acid, which, upon further irradiation, formed a more complex carbon compound, oxalic acid. Both these compounds are important chemicals in certain metabolic activities of the living body. In 1964, Sidney Fox, then at Florida State University and later at the University of Miami, obtained large, stable protein-like macromolecules (termed *proteinoids*) by heating a mixture of 18 protein-forming amino acids to a temperature above the boiling point of water. Equally important, when the proteinoid material was cooled and examined under a microscope, Fox observed small, spherical, cell-like units which arose from aggregations of the proteinoids. These cell-like units, called *microspheres*, were remindful of the living cell. The microspheres are markedly similar to simple bacterial cells.

LIFE'S BEGINNINGS

It is evident that organic compounds can be formed without the intervention of living organisms. Thus, it appears likely that the sea of the primitive earth spontaneously accumulated a great variety of organic molecules. The sea became a sort of dilute organic soup (an "aquatic Garden of Eden"), in which the molecules collided and reacted to form new molecules of increasing levels of complexity. Purines, pyrimidines, nucleotides, and all other constituents of protoplasm came into existence. The association of nucleic acid molecules and proteins would lead inevitably to a virus-like nucleoprotein particle, capable of self-duplication or self-reproduction. The ability of an organism to reproduce its own kind is one of the most fundamental properties of life.

For growth and multiplication, the first living systems drew upon the wealth of organic molecules in the sea broth. Organisms that are dependent upon their environment for their nutritive requirements are called *heterotrophs*. In the primitive world the supply of organic molecules was not inexhaustible. Accordingly, the first heterotrophs could survive only as long as the existing store of organic molecules lasted. Eventually, living systems had to evolve the ability to synthesize their own organic requirements from simple inorganic substances. But a virus-like particle would require a whole array of enzymes to direct a multistep chain of reactions involved in the synthesis of a protein or carbohydrate. It would be too much to expect that all the necessary enzymes evolved at the same time. Norman H. Horowitz of the California Institute of Technology has ingeniously proposed that the chain of steps in a complicated process evolved *backward*.

HOROWITZ'S HYPOTHESIS: BACKWARD EVOLUTION

Horowitz proposed that an organism might acquire, by successive mutations, the enzymes required in a synthetic pathway in the reverse order from that in which they normally appear in a sequence. In other words, evolution began with the end product of the synthetic pathway and worked backward, one step at a time, toward the beginning of the reaction chain. Let us suppose that an organic compound, O, is synthesized through the following steps, where A represents an inorganic substance:

$$A \rightarrow B \rightarrow C \rightarrow D \rightarrow O$$

The first primitive heterotroph, lacking synthetic ability, would require the presence of O in its environment. This essential organic chemical, continually being used by the heterotroph, would eventually become rare, if not exhausted. If a mutation occurred that endowed the heterotroph with the ability to catalyze the reaction from D to O, then the organism would no longer be dependent upon the availability of O in the environment. Indeed, in an environment where O had become depleted, the new mutant would have a survival (selective) advantage over its ancestral type and replace it. As the new mutant reproduced, D in turn would become scarce. Another mutation might occur in the mutant, converting it to a still newer form capable of catalyzing the reaction C to D. At this point, both the first mutant and the newly arisen mutant could live together in a close mutual or symbiotic relationship, establishing the first two-gene system. This unique intimate combination would be able to survive and reproduce in the presence of C or D. As other compounds in the synthetic pathway became progressively rarer, additional mutations for their synthesis would be favorably selected. Ultimately, a multigenic system would evolve capable of directing the synthesis of O from inorganic substance A by way of the intermediate products, B, C, and D. At first glance, it might appear that an unreasonable number of mutational events has been postulated. But it should be recalled that mutations continually occur in living organisms. In fact, the capacity for mutation may be regarded as a supreme property of life.

An organism that possesses the ability to synthesize all of its requirements from simple inorganic substances is termed an *autotroph*. The first simple autotroph lived in an anaerobic world, one in which little, if any, free oxygen was available. The simple autotrophs obtained their energy from chemical reactions, in much the same manner as do present-day bacteria and yeast. The metabolic processes of the primitive anaerobic autotrophs resulted in the liberation of large amounts of carbon dioxide into the atmosphere. Once this occurred, the way was paved for the evolution of organisms which could use carbon dioxide as the sole source of carbon in the synthesis of organic compounds and sunlight as the sole source of energy. Such organisms, of course, would be the photosynthetic green plants. One of the end products of photosynthesis is gaseous oxygen. Thus, for the first time, free oxygen became established in the atmosphere. The presence of free oxygen led to the development of the process of cellular respiration. The processes of photosynthesis and cellular respiration are the twin themes of present-day life.

FOSSILS AND THE HISTORICAL RECORD

Fossils are the remains of organisms preserved or imprinted in the hardened deposits of mud and sand (sedimentary rock) of the earth's crust. Fossils provide documentary evidence for the emergence, throughout the ages, of successively new forms of life with increasing structural complexity. The older strata of rock, those deposited first, bear only relatively simple kinds of life, whereas the newer or younger beds contain progressively more and more complex types of life. Each species of organism now living on the earth has developed from an earlier and simpler ancestral form.

Evidences of life in rocks of great antiquity are steadily accumulating. Masses or beds of limestone, iron ore, and graphite, believed to have been deposited by minute algae and bacteria, occur in deep layers of rock estimated to be 2,700 million years old. One of the most remarkable discoveries of ancient life was reported in 1965 by the paleontologist Elso S. Barghoorn of Harvard University. An electron miscroscope examination of samples of deep sedimentary rock from South Africa revealed the remnants of rod-shaped, bacteria-like organisms, which existed about 3,000 million years ago.

The geologic time scale or calendar of the earth's past history consists of five main divisions, or "eras," associated with five major rock strata, each embracing a number of subdivisions, or "periods." The most ancient era is called the Archeozoic, followed by the Proterozoic, Paleozoic, Mesozoic, and lastly, the Cenozoic, the era of recent types of life. Recognizable

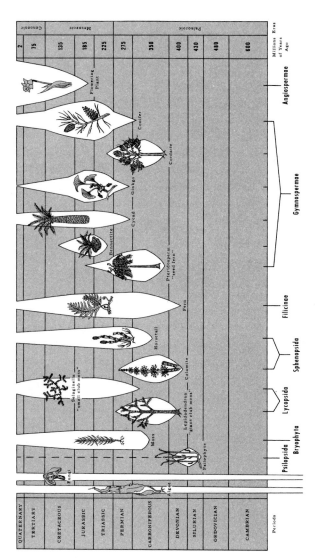

FIG. 14.1. Historical record of plant life. Plant life during the Cambrian and Ordovician, the first two periods of the Paleozoic era, was confined to the water; seaweeds (algae) of immense size, often several hundred feet in length, dominated the seas. Land plants came into existence in Silurian time, in the form of strange little vascular plants, the psilophytes. In the Carboniferous period, imposing spore-bearing trees (Lepidodendrids and Calamites) and primitive naked-seeded plants (Pteridosperms and Cordaites) reached their peak of development. The end of the Paleozoic era marked the extinction of the majority of the luxuriant trees of the Carboniferous coal swamps. The Mesozoic era was the "Age of Gymnosperms," as evidenced by the abundance of cycads, ginkgoes, and conifers. Flowering plants (Angiosperms) rose to ascendancy toward the close of the Mesozoic era and established themselves as the dominant plant group of the earth. The illustration does not reveal the evolutionary relationships between the different plant groups, but each new group that appeared is related to one in the past.

fossils first appear in abundance at the beginning of the Paleozoic era, 600 million years ago. The general character of plant and animal life from the onset of the Paleozoic to recent times is depicted in figures 14.1 and 14.3. Only the broader aspects of past evolution are portrayed. It is evident that the composition of the fauna and flora has changed in the course of geologic time. New types of plants and animals were continually appearing. Some types thrived for a certain time and then disappeared. Others arose and have continued to flourish. Still others have survived until the present day only in very reduced numbers.

In plant history (Fig. 14.1), one of the most significant advances, which occurred in early Paleozoic, was the transition from aquatic existence to life on land. The first plants that established themselves on land were diminutive herbaceous forms, the psilophytes, literally "naked plants," in allusion to their bare, leafless stems. Their existence made possible the subsequent emergence of an infinite variety of tree-sized plants that flourished in the swamps of Carboniferous times. Carboniferous forests included the giant club-moss, *Lepidodendron*, the tall *Calamites*, the coarse-leaved *Cordaites*, and the "seed ferns," *Pteridosperms*, which were the first seed-bearing plants and not true ferns at all. These ancient groups dwindled toward the close of the Paleozoic era and shortly became extinct. Their decomposed remains led to the formation of extensive coal beds throughout

FIG. 14.2. Luxuriant forests of giant trees with dense undergrowth flourished in the Great Coal Age (Carboniferous period), between 350 million and 275 million years ago. The massive trunks at the left are the Lepidodendrids, an extinct group whose modern relatives include the undistinguished small "club mosses" (*Selaginella*) and the "ground pines" (*Lycopodium*). The tall, slender tree with whorled leaves at the right is a Calamite, represented today by a less prominent descendant, the horsetail *Equisetum*. The fernlike plants bearing seeds (at the left) are "seed ferns" (Pteridosperms), which resembled ferns but were actually the first true seed-bearing plants (Gymnosperms). (Courtesy of the Chicago Natural History Museum.)

the world. Figure 14.2 shows the appearance of a Carboniferous swamp as reconstructed from fossils.

By far the greater number of Paleozoic species of plants failed to survive. The Paleozoic flora was largely replaced by the seed-forming gymnosperms, which became prominent in the early Mesozoic era. A diverse assemblage of cycads, ginkgoes (maidenhair trees), and conifers formed elaborate forests. During the closing years of the Mesozoic, the flowering plants (angiosperms), which began very modestly in the Jurassic period, underwent a phenomenal development and constitute today the dominant plants of the earth. The angiosperms have radiated into a variety of habitats, from sea level to mountain summits and from the humid tropics to the dry deserts. Associated with this diversity of habitat is great variety in general form and manner of growth. Many angiosperms have reverted to an aquatic existence. The familiar duckweed, which covers the surface of a pond, is a striking example.

In the animal kingdom, we witness a comparable picture of endless change. The deep Cambrian rocks contain the remains of varied marine invertebrate animals—sponges, jellyfishes, worms, shellfishes, starfishes, and crustaceans (Fig. 14.3). These invertebrates were already so well developed that their differentiation must have taken place during the long Pre-Cambrian period. That this is actually the case has been revealed by the important finding, by the Australian geologists R. C. Sprigg and Martin F. Glaessner, of a rich deposit of Pre-Cambrian fossils in the Ediacara Hills in South Australia. The fossil-bearing rocks lie well below the oldest Cambrian strata, and contain imprints of jellyfishes, tracks of worms, traces of soft corals, and other animals of uncertain nature. Recently, the Dartmouth University geologist Andrew McNair excitingly uncovered Pre-Cambrian remains of invertebrate animals (worms and brachiopods) in rocks, 700 million years old, on Victoria Island in the Canadian arctic.

Dominating the scene in early Paleozoic waters were bizarre arthropods, the trilobites and the large scorpionlike eurypterids. Common in all Paleozoic periods were the nautiloids, related to the modern nautilus, and the brachiopods, or lampshells, relatively inconspicuous today. The odd graptolites, colonial animals whose carbonaceous remains resemble pencil marks, attained the peak of their development in the Ordovician period and then abruptly declined. No land animals are known for Cambrian and Ordovician times. Seascapes of the early Paleozoic are shown in Figure 14.4.

Many of the prominent Paleozoic marine invertebrate groups became extinct or declined sharply in numbers before the advent of the Mesozoic era. During the Mesozoic, shelled ammonoids flourished in the seas and insects and reptiles were the predominant land forms. At the close of the

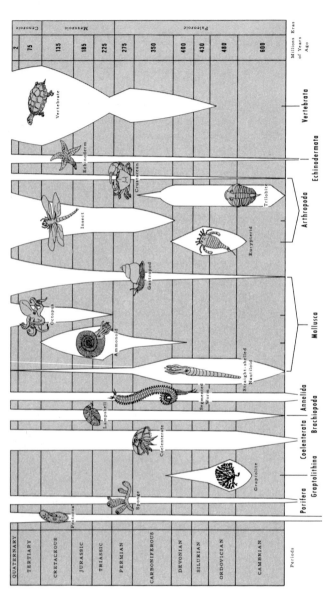

FIG. 14.3. Historical record of animal life. Many of the invertebrate groups were already highly diversified and abundant in the Cambrian, the first period of the Paleozoic era, approximately 600 million years ago. The Paleozoic era is often called the "Age of Invertebrates," with its multitude of nautiloids, eurypterids, and trilobites. Brachiopods with hinged valves were the commonest shellfish of the Paleozoic seas. In the Mesozoic era, air-breathing insects and vertebrates, notably the widely distributed reptiles (see Fig. 12.4), held the center of the stage. The Mesozoic seas were populated with large, shelled ammonoids, now extinct. Warm-blooded vertebrates (birds and mammals) became prominent in the Cenozoic era, and man himself arrived on the scene in the closing stages of this era (see chapter 15).

FIG. 14.4. Highly diversified assemblage of invertebrates of early Paleozoic seas. *Top:* Ordovician period. Large organism in foreground is a straight-shelled nautiloid. Other prominent forms are trilobites, massive corals, smaller nautiloids, and a snail. *Bottom:* Cambrian period. Conspicuous animals are the trilobite (center foreground), eurypterid (center background), and the jellyfish (left). Other animals include brachiopods, annelid worms, sea cucumber, and varied shelled forms. (*Top,* courtesy of Chicago National History Museum; *Bottom,* courtesy of the American Museum of Natural History.)

Mesozoic, the once successful marine ammonoids perished and the reptilian dynasty collapsed, giving way to the birds and mammals. Insects have continued to thrive and have differentiated into a staggering variety of species. Well over 600,000 different species of insects have been described, and conservative estimates place the total number of living species today at 3 million.

During the course of evolution, plant and animal groups interacted to each other's advantage. There is little doubt, for example, that the rise and spread of flowering plants fostered the diversification and dispersal of insects. As flowering plants became less and less dependent on wind for pollination, a great variety of insects emerged as specialists in transporting pollen. The colors and fragrances of flowers evolved as adaptations to attract insects. Flowering plants also exerted a major influence on the evolution of birds and mammals. Birds, which feed on seeds, fruits, and buds, evolved rapidly in intimate association with the flowering plants. The emergence of herbivorous mammals coincided with the widespread distribution of nutritious grasses over the plains during the Cenozoic era. In turn, the herbivorous mammals furnished the setting for the evolution of carnivorous mammals. The interdependency between plants and animals continues to exist in nature today.

EVOLUTIONARY STABILITY

The multitude of different kinds of present-day organisms is impressive. Yet, the inhabitants of the world today are but a small percent of the tremendous array of organisms of prior periods. As we have seen, the fate of most lineages of organisms in the course of time is extinction. Apparently, only those populations that can continue to adapt to changing environmental conditions avoid extinction. Yet some types of organisms have not changed appreciably in untold millions of years. A long-standing stability of organization seems antithetical to the concept of evolution. The opossum has survived almost unchanged since late Cretaceous, some 75 or more million years ago. The horseshoe crab, *Limulus*, is not very different from fossils uncovered some 500 million years ago. The maidenhair, or ginkgo, tree of the Chinese temple gardens differs little from its ancestors 200 million years back. The treasured ginkgo has probably existed on earth longer than any other tree that is now living. Darwin called the ginkgo "a living fossil." We have no adequate explanation for such unexpected stability of organization. Perhaps some organisms have reached an almost perfect adjustment to a relatively unchanging environment. One thing, however, is certain: such stable forms are not at all dominant in our present-day world. One of the dominant forms today, which we shall discuss in the next chapter, is man, a mammal that has evolved rapidly in a relatively short span of years.

SUGGESTIONS FOR FURTHER READING

ADLER, I. 1957. *How life began.* New York: New American Library of World Literature, Inc.

BUCHSBAUM, R. 1948. *Animals without backbones.* Chicago: University of Chicago Press.

DeBEER, G. 1964. *Atlas of evolution.* London: Thomas Nelson & Sons.

GLAESSNER, M. F. 1961. Pre-Cambrian animals. *Scientific American,* March, pp. 72–78.

KEOSIAN, J. 1964. *The origin of life.* New York: Reinhold Publishing Corp.

MILLER, S. L. 1953. A production of amino acids under possible primitive earth conditions. *Science* 117:528–529.

OPARIN, A. I. 1953. *The origin of life.* New York: Dover Publications, Inc.

ROMER, A. S. 1959. *The vertebrate story.* Chicago: University of Chicago Press.

SIMPSON, G. G. 1953. *Life of the past.* New Haven: Yale University Press.

STIRTON, R. A. 1959. *Time, life, and man.* New York: John Wiley & Sons, Inc.

WALD, G. 1954. The origin of life. *Scientific American,* August, pp. 44–53.

WALTON, J. 1953. *An introduction to the study of fossil plants.* London: A. & C. Black, Ltd.

15

Emergence
of Man

Man has unique attributes, but he is an animal and the product of the same natural evolutionary forces that have shaped other forms of animal life. There is almost universal unanimity that the closest relatives of man are the apes. The line leading ultimately to man diverged from the ape branch during Tertiary times. There are several candidates among Tertiary fossil manlike apes that qualify for the position ancestral to man. One often hears stated, hesitatingly and perhaps in the form of an apology, that man is not really a descendant of the apes but merely shares a very distant ancestry with the apes. By indirection, the evasive idea is conveyed that our remote generalized ancestor would not be at all apelike. This is sheer deception. There is simply no blinking the question that modern man's ancestors were apelike, and that the human family did indeed branch off from the ape line.

PRIMATE RADIATION

The primates, the order to which man belongs, underwent adaptive radiation when they first arose in Cenozoic times, approximately 75 million years ago. The primates are primarily tree dwellers; only man is fully adapted for life on the ground. Many of the noteworthy characteristics of the primates evolved as specializations for an arboreal mode of life. Depth perception is important to a tree-living animal; the majority of the primates are unique in possessing binocular or stereoscopic vision, wherein the visual fields of the two eyes overlap. The hands evolved as organs for grasping, manipulating, and exploring objects. Closely associated with the development of great visual acuity and increased dexterity of the hands was the marked expansion of the brain. Progressive enlargement of the brain culminated, in man, in the development of higher mental faculties.

From small, chisel-tooth, insectivorous ancestors, the primate stock arose and differentiated along varied lines (Fig. 15.1). One of the branches

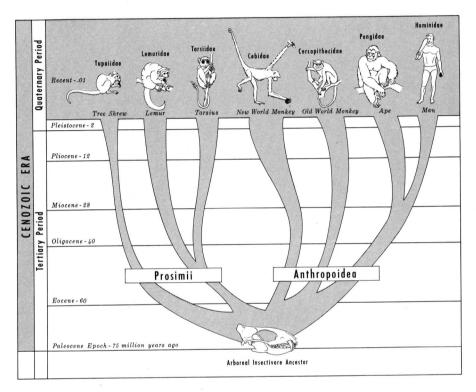

FIG. 15.1. Adaptive radiation of the primates from a basic stock of small, insect-eating placental mammals, the Insectivora (whose living kin include the shrews, moles, and hedgehogs). The primitive Primate families (Tupaiidae, Lemuridae, and Tarsiidae) are grouped together in the suborder Prosimii; the more advanced families (Cebidae, Cercopithecidae, Pongidae, and Hominidae) are assigned to the suborder Anthropoidea. The pongid (ape) and hominid (man) lineages diverged during the Miocene epoch.

is represented today by the primitive Oriental tree shrew, *Tupaia*, an agile tree climber that feeds on insects and fruits in tropical forests. Once widely distributed but now mostly confined to the forests of Madagascar are the lemurs, small timid creatures with sharp, foxlike muzzles. A step above the lemurs in the scale of primate evolution is the nocturnal, arboreal *Tarsius*, found in the East Indies. The more advanced primates comprise the New World monkeys, the Old World monkeys, the great apes, and man. All are able to sit in an upright position, and thus the hands are free to manipulate objects. The monkeys are normally quadrupedal, walking on all fours; the apes are efficient brachiators, using their arms for hand-over-hand swinging or climbing; and man alone is specialized for erect bipedal locomotion.

The anatomical features which distinguish modern man from the living apes are comparatively few. The resemblances in skeletal structures, muscular anatomy, physiological processes, serological reactions, and chromosome patterns are all strikingly close. The pronounced differences relate mainly to locomotor habits and brain growth. Man has a fully up-right posture and gait, and an enlarged brain (mean cranial capacity of about 1,350 cubic centimeters). Much of man's mastery of varied environments has been the result of his superior intelligence, gradually acquired in the course of evolution.

When we speak of man, we inevitably think of him as he exists today. Present-day man is certainly different from his predecessors, in much the same manner that the modern horse is different from his forerunners. Thus, when a Pleistocene fossil specimen is designated as an "ape-man" or a "near-man," it should not be imagined that such an extinct form possessed the qualities of man as we know him today. It is important to recognize that there have been different kinds of men. The evolutionary process of adaptive radiation had led to a family of men, recognized formally as the Hominidae, of which modern man—*Homo sapiens*, or "man the wise" —is only one member and the sole survivor.

FOSSIL PRE-MAN

Fragmentary remains have been uncovered of apelike primates that inhabited the Old World during Miocene and early Pliocene times, about 25 million to 10 million years ago (Fig. 15.2). Most are clearly members of the ape family (Pongidae), such as *Pliopithecus*, a Miocene gibbon-like creature that is generally regarded as ancestral to today's gibbons. Miocene sediments of Europe and Asia, especially India, have yielded teeth and jaws of *Dryopithecus*, the "oak-ape," so called because of the presence of oak leaves in the fossil deposits. These primitive oak-apes were the early forerunners of the modern orangutan, chimpanzee, and gorilla. A fossil form that once aroused lively debate is *Oreopithecus*, unearthed in Italian coal beds which date back to the early Pliocene, approximately 10 million years ago. In the 1950's, the Swiss scholar Johannes Hurzeler championed the view that *Oreopithecus* is a primitive hominid in the direct line of man's ancestry. The consensus of current thought is that *Oreopithecus* is an aberrant offshoot of the pongid stock that disappeared without issue (Fig. 15.2).

Some Miocene apelike types seem to be close to the lineage of man. One of these is *Proconsul africanus*, discovered in the 1930's by the vet-

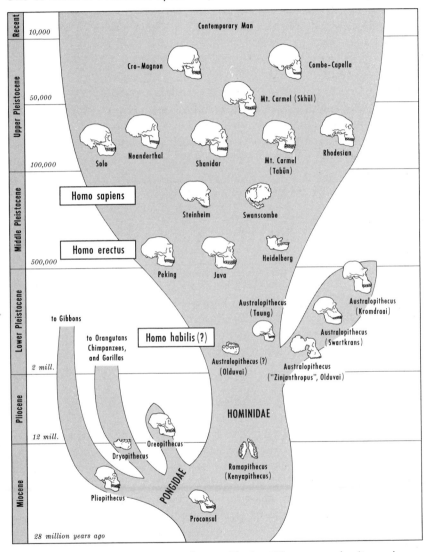

FIG. 15.2. Geologic past of man. The late Miocene epoch witnessed the separation of the pongid (ape) and hominid (man) assemblages. The evolution of man was not limited to a single lineage. Several branches forked off from the main stem and were not directly ancestral to modern man, *Homo sapiens*.

eran archaeologist Louis Leakey, on an island in Lake Victoria, Kenya. *Proconsul* is known by a nearly complete cranium, numerous teeth and jaw fragments, and several limb bones. The anatomical features of the skull and dentition are remarkably unspecialized for an ape. The generalized skeletal characteristics suggest that *Proconsul* is not far removed from the common stock from which apes and men arose. *Proconsul africanus* is believed to have been a slender and agile creature, more monkey-like than apelike. He was primarily a tree dweller, but apparently he descended on many occasions to the ground. The transition from tree-dwelling to ground-living might well have first appeared at this time. In the Miocene epoch, the great expanse of tropical rain forest in East Africa dwindled, leaving patches of wooded valleys separated by open bushy grasslands. The capacity for ground walking may have evolved as an adaptation enabling arboreal forms to cross the open plains in passing from one patch of woodland to another. Thus, *Proconsul* may have become a ground dweller in order to continue to live successfully in the trees. This is a seeming paradox, parallel to the intriguing conjecture, earlier discussed, that water-living vertebrates evolved terrestrial habits in order to retain, and not abandon, their aquatic mode of life.

In the 1960's, the Leakeys (Louis Leakey and his accomplished wife, Mary) made a dramatic find in East Africa. An upper jaw, with unmistakable hominid dentition, was found at Kenya in deposits of a geological age of 14 million years. This fragmentary specimen was named *Kenyapithecus*, although it is basically similar to the remains of an upper jaw of a Miocene form, known as *Ramapithecus*, which was found in 1935 by G. Edward Lewis in the Siwalik Hills of northern India. *Kenyapithecus*, now equated with *Ramapithecus*, apparently ranged widely throughout Africa and Asia in late Miocene and early Pliocene times. This fossil type may be close to the base of the stem of the hominid family. That is to say, *Ramapithecus* may mark the point where the hominid lineage separated from the pongid assemblage (Fig. 15.2). Several authors accept *Ramapithecus* as the earliest member of the family of men (Hominidae). The hominid status implies that *Ramapithecus* was bipedal and ventured into open country to forage for food. The roots of man's family tree apparently date back 20 million years.

APE-MEN OR NEAR-MEN

In 1924, an epochal discovery in South Africa was announced by Raymond Dart, an Australian anatomist at the University of Witwatersrand in Johannesburg. In a Pleistocene limestone quarry near the small village of Taung in Bechuanaland was found the fossilized skull of a juvenile, corresponding to that of a child of about six years. The little Taung skull bears some resemblance to that of a young chimpanzee, but many of its components, notably the teeth, show pronounced affinities to man. Dart named the remarkable skull *Australopithecus africanus*, and asserted that it was related to the ancestral stock of man rather than to the great apes (Fig. 15.2). In other words, the Taung fossil represented an early member of the Hominidae, the family of man, rather than of the Pongidae, the family of apes.

Dart's declaration, initially vigorously refuted by a number of scientists, was fortified by findings in the 1930's by the late Robert Broom, a distinguished paleontologist of Scottish origin. Adult skulls of *Australopithecus* were dug out from caves in Sterkfontein, Kromdraai, and Swartkrans in South Africa. The adult skulls realized closely the structural features inferred from the juvenile Taung cranium. The several new fossil forms were originally given different names. However, in recent years, it has become customary to refer to the South African ape-men collectively as the Australopithecines. They were short in stature, four to five feet in height, with a brain capacity (about 600 cubic centimeters) barely exceeding that of a modern gorilla (510 cubic centimeters). Nonetheless, the Australopithecines stood upright, walked bipedally, and dwelt in open country. These circumstances nullify the popular view that man was an intelligent animal when he first came down out of the trees. It seems clear that erect bipedal locomotion on the ground preceded the development of a large complex brain.

The Australopithecines are decidedly early representatives of the hominid lineage. However, there is spirited debate as to whether the Australopithecines represent an evolutionary blind alley in man's ancestry or occupy a prominent place in the direct ancestry of man. In 1959, Louis and Mary Leakey discovered a unique lower Pleistocene hominid in the deep eroding slopes of the Olduvai Gorge in Tanzania of East Africa. The heavy-jawed fossil form was called *Zinjanthropus*, or the Nutcracker Man (Fig. 15.2). Fossil remains of *Zinjanthropus* were found in strata dated by a new potassium-argon method (instead of the conventional uranium-lead technique) to be about one and three-quarter million years old.

The discovery of crude tools fabricated out of pebbles in association with the remains of *Zinjanthropus* led initially to the belief that this early hominid was a toolmaker. However, the prevailing opinion is that the stone tools were not made by *Zinjanthropus*, but were rather the work of another, more advanced kind of hominid found at the same level as *Zinjanthropus* in the Olduvai strata. This more advanced hominid was a small, light-jawed form, with a cranial capacity (680 cubic centimeters) greater than that of *Zinjanthropus* or any of the Australopithecines. Some anthropologists argue that the light-jawed form constituted the first "civilized" or "humanized" man, deserving of the rank of *Homo*, namely *Homo habilis*. The specific name *habilis* means "able, handy, mentally skillful, vigorous," from the inferred ability of this man to make stone tools. Thus, *Homo habilis* would bridge the gap between the Australopithecines, which had not acquired human status, and Java man (*Homo erectus*), which had attained human status (Fig. 15.2). The recognition of *Homo habilis* indicates that this primitive human being was evolving alongside, and lived side-by-side with, the less hominized Australopithecines.

The co-existence of *Homo habilis* and the Australopithecines has been the subject of much concern among anthropologists. Some writers contend that *Homo habilis* did not cross the threshold between the pre-human and human grades, and represented only an advanced member of the Australopithecines. Under this view, there existed two contemporaneous species of *Australopithecus* in eastern Africa in the early Pleistocene—the heavy-jawed *Australopithecus robustus* (otherwise known as *Zinjanthropus*) and the more advanced light-jawed *Australopithecus africanus* (otherwise known as *Homo habilis*). If the two *Australopithecus* species did coexist at the same time in the same region, then only one of the two could have been the progenitor of a more modern species of man. The available evidence suggests that *Australopithecus robustus* perished without leaving any descendants, and that *Australopithecus africanus* (or *Homo habilis* of some authors) was the forebear of the more modern *Homo erectus*.

EARLY TRUE MAN

The famous Java man, first described as *Pithecanthropus erectus*, undoubtedly had crossed the threshold between pre-human and human grades (Fig. 15.2). This primitive human being was discovered at Trinil, Java in 1894 by Eugène Dubois, a young Dutch army surgeon. Dubois had been profoundly influenced by the writings of Charles Darwin, and had become inbued with the idea that he could find the origins of man in the Far East. He surprised the world with the discovery of the earliest human. Curiously, Dubois, in his later years, inexplicably doubted his own finding and contended that *Pithecanthropus erectus* was merely a giant manlike ape. In the 1930's additional fossil finds of *Pithecanthropus* were unearthed in central Java by the Dutch anthropologist G. H. R. von Koenigswald. The new findings confirmed the human status of *Pithecanthropus*.

Java man lived during middle Pleistocene times, between 500,000 and 300,000 years ago (Fig. 15.2). This low-browed man was a toolmaker and a hunter who had learned to use fire. He most likely had some powers of speech. Java man's ability to exploit his environment is reflected in the expanded size of his brain. The brain cavity had a capacity of 770 to 1,000 cubic centimeters.

In the 1920's elaborate excavations undertaken by the Canadian anatomist Davidson Black of caves in the limestone hills near Peking, China, led to the discovery of another primitive man, *Sinanthropus pekinensis*, or Peking man. The cranial capacity in Peking man varied from 900 to 1200 cubic centimeters. He fashioned tools and weapons of stone and bone and kindled fire. There is a strong suspicion that Peking man was cannibalistic and savoured human brains, for many of the fossil braincases show signs of having been cracked open from below.

Java man and Peking man were originally each christened with a distinctive Latin name, *Pithecanthropus erectus* and *Sinanthropus pekinensis*, respectively. There is, however, no justification for recognizing more than the single genus of humans, *Homo*. Accordingly, modern taxonomists have properly assigned both Java man and Peking man to the genus *Homo*. Moreover, the morphological differences between these two fossil men are readily within the range of variation that we observe in living populations today. These forms, therefore, represent two closely related geographic races (subspecies) of the same species. Lastly, both Java and Peking men are distinct enough from modern man (*Homo sapiens*) to warrant being placed together in a different species, *Homo erectus*.

These nomenclatural changes may appear to be trivial, but the implications are great. One important implication is that human populations at any one time period were differentiated into geographical races, not into distinct species or even genera. We can envision, for example, that approximately 500,000 years ago, there existed a single widespread species of man, with eastern populations being represented by the Java and Peking variants and the western populations being constituted by types resembling Heidelberg man (found in an early Pleistocene sand deposit near Heidelberg, Germany). The suspected wide distribution of *Homo erectus* has been confirmed by the recent discoveries of this early type of man in North Africa (Ternifine, Algeria) and East Africa (Olduvai Gorge, Tanzania). Evidently, then, populations of *Homo erectus* had spread successfully through the continents, from the tropical regions of Africa to southeast Asia.

EMERGENCE OF MODERN MAN

The classic Neanderthal man was first unearthed in 1856 in a limestone cave in the Neander ravine near Düsseldorf, Germany (Fig. 15.3). It is one of the best known of fossil men, having been subsequently found at numerous widely separate sites in Europe, particularly in France. The half-brutish Neanderthal man was a cave-dweller, short (about 5 feet) but powerfully built, with prominent facial brow ridges, and a large brain with an average capacity of 1,450 cubic centimeters (as opposed to 1,350 cubic centimeters in modern man). Neanderthal man first arose some 100,-

000 years ago. He roamed over Europe up to about 40,000 years ago (Upper Pleistocene), and then he dramatically disappeared. He was replaced by men of a modern type, much like ourselves, which have been grouped under the common name of Cro-Magnon.

The transition from Neanderthal man to Cro-Magnon man is problematical. Prior to the time of the Neanderthalers themselves, about 200,000 to 100,000 years ago, there emerged types of men, such as Swanscombe from England and Steinheim from Germany, that did not conform to the classic Neanderthal type. Indeed, the Swanscombe and Steinheim skulls (Fig. 15.2) are not markedly different from that of modern man. Is it possible that a modern type of man arose before Neanderthal? We have grown accustomed to the idea that Neanderthal man was our direct ancestor, but now it appears that we may be closer to the truth by considering him as a sterile offshoot. The picture, however, is far from clear. In the Middle East about 100,000 to 30,000 years ago there existed an exceptionally heterogeneous group of men. These are represented by the Palestinian Mount Carmel man, dug out of caves at Tabūn and Skhūl, and the Shanidar man, excavated from caves in the mountains of northern Iraq (Fig. 15.2).

FIG. 15.3. Reconstruction of the appearance of Neanderthal man, a rugged cave-dweller who roamed Europe and the Middle East about 75,000 years ago. [Painting by Maurice Wilson; by permission of the British Museum (Natural History)].

These men ranged from individuals with almost typical western European Neanderthal features to those that are barely distinguishable from modern man. We shall comment again on this Middle East variable community of men in a subsequent section.

Another element of uncertainty is the relationship of the European Neanderthal man to other Upper Pleistocene men in widely scattered parts of the world—Rhodesian man of central Africa and Solo man of Java (Fig. 15.2). Rhodesian and Solo men have been considered by some authorities to be the geographical equivalents of Neanderthal man of Europe. This, of course, would lead us to believe that the classic Neanderthal man was widely distributed in the Old World. Below we shall attempt to unravel some of these knotty problems.

STATUS OF NEANDERTHAL MAN

There is no complete agreement among authorities on the status of Neanderthal man. As we have already noted, the populations of Neanderthal man in Europe disappeared rather abruptly and were replaced by a modern group (Cro-Magnon) that definitely belongs of *Homo sapiens*. Does this indicate that two separate species, *Homo neanderthalensis* and *Homo sapiens*, actually existed together in Europe, and that the latter species displaced the former without hybridization occurring between the two? Perceptive views on this question have been expressed by the evolutionist Theodosius Dobzhansky, formerly of Columbia University and later at Rockefeller University in New York. Dobzhansky calls attention to the Mount Carmel fossil populations in Palestine, particularly that found at Skhūl. This extraordinary fossil assemblage consists of individuals ranging from classical European Neanderthal types to forms closely resembling *Homo sapiens*. This suggests a racial mixture of the two groups. It would appear, then, that the European Neanderthal men and the Middle East modern men were not reproductively incompatible, as would be two species, but rather were races of the same species (*Homo sapiens*). In other words, the Mount Carmel locality represented a zone of integradation of a kind usually found at the boundaries of geographic races (see chapter 9). The emergence of Cro-Magnon man may have resulted, at least to some extent, from the amalgamation of the European Neanderthal race and the Middle East modern-like race invading Europe.

Although this interpretation seems reasonable, there are authorities who claim that the classic Neanderthalers were not directly involved in the ancestry of modern man. Clark Howell, professor of anthropology at Chicago University, suggests that little, if any, opportunity existed for the exchange of genes between the Neanderthal populations of western Europe and those in the Middle East or elsewhere. During the Pleistocene epoch many parts of Europe were covered with sheets of glacial ice. It may be that the Neanderthalers of western Europe were geographically isolated by the Ice Age of 100,000 years ago. Neanderthal man may have perished in isolation before modern man arrived, or may have been overrun by their more progressive Middle East contemporaries who had spread into Western Europe. Under this viewpoint, Neanderthal man represented an evolutionary dead-end in man's ancestry. Modern man evolved independently of Neanderthal man, and arose by separate origin via the middle Pleistocene *sapiens*-like stock—Steinheim man and Swanscombe man (Fig. 15.4) —and the more advanced Mount Carmel men in Upper Pleistocene.

FIG. 15.4. Reconstruction of the life of Swanscombe man from England, one of the earliest members of *Homo sapiens*. Swanscombe man spread across the plains of northern Europe about 200,000 to 100,000 years ago. [Painting by Maurice Wilson; by permission of the British Museum (Natural History)].

Cro-Magnon man, a representative of our own species, *Homo sapiens*, can be traced back to about 35,000 years ago. His remains have been found in many sites in western and central Europe. The Cro-Magnon men showed individual differences, just as man today exhibits individual variation. One of the notable variants is Combe-Capelle man from France (Fig. 15.2).

Little is known of modern man in other continents during the time that Cro-Magnon flourished in Europe. This does not mean that the Cro-Magnon type originated in Europe. Modern man may have been cradled in Asia or Africa.

ORIGIN OF RACES OF MAN

We do not know the birthplace of modern man. Nevertheless, we do *not* believe that Cro-Magnon man originated simultaneously in widely different parts of the world. Rather he arose in one place, then migrated to various regions of the globe and became differentiated into geographical races. This is the orthodox and established pattern of geographical origin of races (see chapter 9.) There is, however, a school of thought, chiefly identified with Franz Weidenreich and Carleton Coon, that conceives of the modern races of man as descending from different ancient hominid lineages evolving independently of one another. Thus, as seen in Figure 15.5, Java man was the early progenitor of the Australoid race; Peking

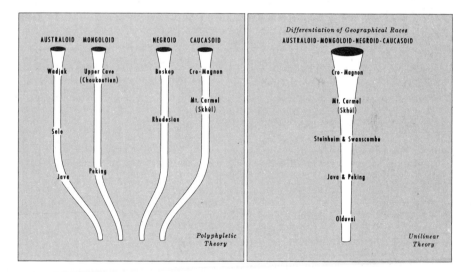

FIG. 15.5. Racial origins of man. The polyphyletic hypothesis envisions a distant separation of the principal races of man. The four basic races had evolved independently and in parallel fashion over hundreds of thousands of years. This startling thesis that the primary races of mankind can be traced far back in prehistoric antiquity is scarcely defensible in light of modern evolutionary concepts. The recent origin of the living races of man, as expressed by the unilinear theory, is soundly tenable. Racial differentiation occurred only after modern man (Cro-Magnon) arose and became distributed over a large area of the world.

man was the forerunner of the Mongoloid race; Rhodesian man gave rise ultimately to the Negroid race; and a Middle East type, perhaps Mount Carmel, led to the Caucasoid race. Accordingly, the races of man are virtually older than the species, *Homo sapiens*, itself.

An illustration of the principle of parallel evolution was given in chapter 13, where we observed that the New World and Old World porcupines followed independent, but parallel, courses of evolutionary development. But, by no stretch of the imagination could the South American and African porcupines be considered as racial variants of one species. These two porcupine groups are certainly reproductively incompatible. The Weidenreich-Coon School would argue that geographic separation of the different hominid branches did not lead to reproductive isolation, as might be expected of populations of long standing that are spatially separated and differentiate along independent lines. It is, however, exceedingly difficult to imagine how several hominid races, diverging in different parts of the world, can evolve independently and yet repeatedly in the same direction leading only to one species, *Homo sapiens*. The parallel origin of races is not hopelessly out of the question, but if it occurs, it must be the very exception to the normal process. Indeed, modern evolutionists are disposed to relegate the Weidenreich-Coon notion of parallel evolution of races to the category of the highly improbable.

There seems little doubt that *Homo sapiens* originated in a single area, then spread the world over and differentiated into the basic races of mankind (see Fig. 9.4). The races of man, once geographically separated to a large extent, have intermingled and intercrossed for untold thousands of years. The distinguishing features of the basic racial groups have become increasingly blurred by the countless migrations and intermixings. The whole world today is a single large neighborhood. Contemporary man lives in one great reproductive community.

Suggestions for Further Reading

Bleibtreu, H. K. (ed.) 1969. *Evolutionary anthropology.* Boston: Allyn and Bacon, Inc.

Campbell, B. G. 1966. *Human evolution.* Chicago: Aldine Publishing Co.

Clark, W. E. LeGros. 1961. *History of the primates.* Chicago: University of Chicago Press.

———. 1964. *The fossil evidence for human evolution.* Chicago: University of Chicago Press.

Dart, R. and Craig, D. 1959. *Adventures with the missing link.* New York: Harper & Row, Publishers.

Dobzhansky, T. 1960. The present evolution of man. *Scientific American,* September, pp. 206–217.

———. 1962. *Mankind evolving.* New Haven: Yale University Press.

HOWELL, F. C. and Editors of *Life*. 1965. *Early man*. New York: Time, Inc. Book Division.

HOWELLS, W. W. 1959. *Mankind in the making*. New York: Doubleday & Co., Inc.

—————. 1960. The distribution of man. *Scientific American*, September, pp. 112–127.

HUXLEY, T. H. 1959. *Man's place in nature*. Ann Arbor: University of Michigan Press.

LEAKEY, L. S. B. 1960. *Adam's ancestors*. New York: Harper & Row, Publishers.

MEDAWAR, P. B. 1961. *The future of man*. New York: New American Library of World Literature, Inc.

MONTAGU, A. 1961. *Man in process*. New York: New American Library of World Literature, Inc.

—————. 1962. *Man: his first million years*. New York: New American Library of World Literature, Inc.

WASHBURN, S. L. 1960. Tools and human evolution. *Scientific American*, September, pp. 62–75.

Epilogue

Man's Progress and Prospect

Modern man has a double heritage. He is a product of both biological and cultural evolution. Human culture has emerged out of man's exercise of reason and his ability to communicate his rational thoughts. Man's cultural endowments supplement and transcend his purely biological inheritance. The child is born uncivilized, and acquires his customs, beliefs, and values by instruction and imitation. Each new generation is able to draw upon the rich store of past accumulated knowledge and ideas.

Through his capacity to absorb, transmit, and modify the body of learned tradition known as culture, man has been able to reach beyond himself. In contrast to other animals, he can imagine and plan. There are no rigidly fixed limits to what he can make out of life and to what he can create. Considering these facts, it seems inevitable that man is uncertain about his limitations, and hence, sets his goals either too high or too low. His ambivalence concerning his goals forever plagues him.

Man has gained a large measure of control over his environment. He is no longer completely at nature's mercy. He has exploited and tamed nature to a degree that he lives for the most part in an environment of his own creation. He has been eminently successful in molding nature for his own ends. But it is clear that man is only part master of the world in which he lives. While knowledge and the advances of science have broadened his command over nature, he still is unable to govern either himself or his environment. He remains dependent on his fellow man and their benevolent concern for his survival, as well as the impersonal forces of nature that are entirely outside his control. The growing concern about the problems of the environment—air, water, and noise pollution—emanates from the fact that man has failed to treat nature with respect. Nature can exist without man, but man cannot exist without nature.

166

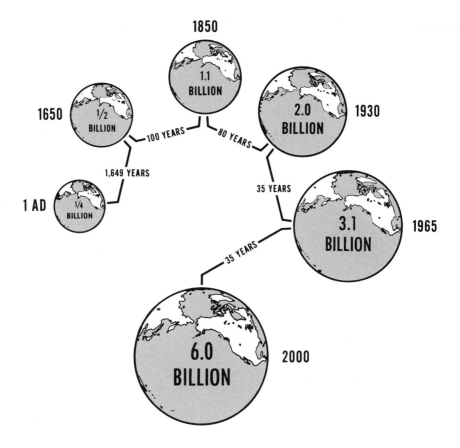

A rapidly swelling population threatens the existence of mankind. Population increase is a luxury that man can no longer afford.

Man has not learned to manage himself. He has admirably reduced his mortality rate and has prolonged his life span, but he has yet to voluntarily restrict his explosive birth rate. Man today is multiplying in great numbers. The knotty problem of global overpopulation must be resolved by means other than war and famine. As shown in the pictorial diagram, the world population at the birth of the Christian era is estimated at 250 million people. It took approximately 1,750 years for the total population to reach the one billion mark in 1850. Within 80 years, from 1850 to 1930, the population had doubled to 2 billion. By 1965, the population had reached 3.1 billion—an increase of more than one billion in the short span of 35 years. The world population is now growing by 2 percent per year, which means that *every day* there are 180,000 more people on the earth.

At this rate, the forecast by the year 2000 is 6 billion people. Quite obviously, the phenomenal population growth, or rather explosion, cannot continue unchecked.

So rapid has been the acceleration in growth that half the population now living on the earth has been born since 1945. An increasing number of young people are moving into the reproductive ages. The number of women in the high-fertility age group (20–30 years old) will increase by approximately a half in the next 20 years. This enlarging "fertility potential" adds dramatically to the gravity of the population crisis. A population increase is a luxury that man can no longer afford. A *zero* population growth rate—one in which births balance deaths—is not only a desideratum, but an essential necessity. Such stabilization of the population calls for an average family size of 2.3 children. This is the number that, multiplied by the number of child-bearing families, would provide just enough new individuals to balance those who pass away.

Man is the most successful product of evolution. But his future survival is not inevitable or assured by any known natural law. Indeed, as we have seen, a cardinal theme of evolution is that most species of organisms eventually decline and pass out of existence. Many urgent problems bedevil mankind. Man may stumble along and blunder himself into oblivion. It would be vastly better, of course, for man to use his great intellect to avoid, or at least postpone, extinction.

SUGGESTIONS FOR FURTHER READING

BRESLER, JACK B. (ed.) 1968. *Environments of man.* Reading, Mass.: Addison-Wesley Publishing Co.

BROWN, H. 1954. *The challenge of man's future.* New York: The Viking Press, Inc.

CARSON, R. 1962. *Silent spring.* Boston: Houghton Mifflin Co.

COMMONER, B. C. 1967. *Science and survival.* New York: The Viking Press.

DRAPER, E. 1965. *Birth control in the modern world.* Baltimore, Md.: Penguin Books Ltd.

DUBOS, R. 1968. *So human an animal.* New York: Charles Scribner's Sons.

EHRLICH, P. R. 1968. *The population bomb.* New York: Ballantine Books.

HARDIN, G. 1969. *Population, evolution, and birth control.* San Francisco: W. H. Freeman & Co., Publishers.

JOHNSON, CECIL E. (ed.) 1968. *Social and natural biology.* Princeton, N. J.: D. Van Nostrand Co., Inc.

KORMONDY, E. J. 1969. *Concepts of ecology.* Englewood Cliffs, N. J.: Prentice-Hall, Inc.

LERNER, I. M. 1968. *Heredity, evolution, and society.* San Francisco: W. H. Freeman & Co., Publishers.

LORENZ, K. 1963. *On aggression.* London: Methuen & Co. Ltd.

PADDOCK, W. and PADDOCK, P. 1967. *Famine—1975!* Boston: Little, Brown and Co.

RUDD, R. L. 1966. *Pesticides and the living landscape*. Madison, Wisc.: University of Wisconsin Press.

SHEPARD, P. and McKINLEY, D. 1969. *The subversive science*. Boston: Houghton Mifflin Co.

TAYLOR, G. R. 1968. *The biological time bomb*. Cleveland, Ohio: The World Publishing Co.

WHYTE, W. H. 1968. *The last landscape*. Garden City, N.Y.: Doubleday & Co., Inc.

Index

(Page numbers in bold face refer to illustrations.)